MILTON

The Sacred Art of the World

Samuel Bercholz, Editor
Carolyn Rose, Associate Editor

WILLIAM BLAKE
MILTON

Edited and with a Commentary by
KAY PARKHURST EASSON
and
ROGER R. EASSON

SHAMBHALA · BOULDER
in association with
RANDOM HOUSE · NEW YORK
1978

SHAMBHALA PUBLICATIONS, INC.
1123 SPRUCE STREET
BOULDER, COLORADO 80302
In association with
RANDOM HOUSE, INC.
NEW YORK, NEW YORK 10022

THIS BOOK IS PUBLISHED IN COOPERATION WITH
THE AMERICAN BLAKE FOUNDATION
AT MEMPHIS STATE UNIVERSITY
COMMENTARY © 1978 THE AMERICAN BLAKE FOUNDATION

LIBRARY OF CONGRESS CATALOGING IN PUBLICATION DATA

Blake, William, 1757-1827   Milton.
(The Sacred Art of the World)

1. Milton, John, 1608-1674, in fiction, drama,
poetry, etc.   I.   Easson, Kay.   II.   Easson, Roger R.
III. Title.
PR4144.M6   1978b   821'.7   78-58177
ISBN 0-394-50300-7   ISBN 0-394-73630-3   pbk.

PRINTED IN THE UNITED STATES OF AMERICA

For Winston Weathers

Acknowledgments

Copy B of *Milton* is reproduced here by kind permission of
The Henry E. Huntington Library and Art Gallery, San Marino, California.

Plates a-f of Copy D of *Milton* are reproduced here by kind permission
of The Lessing J. Rosenwald Collection of the Library of Congress,
Alverthorpe Gallery, Jenkintown, Pennsylvania.

Figures 2, 3, and 5 in the Commentary are taken from the Rees *Cyclopædia*,
which is in The Collection of The American Blake Foundation.

CONTENTS

PART ONE
PLATES

To Justify the Ways of God to Men

PREFACE.

The Stolen and Perverted Writings of Homer &
Ovid: of Plato & Cicero. which all Men ought to
contemn: are set up by artifice against the Sublime
of the Bible, but when the New Age is at leisure
to Pronounce; all will be set right & those Grand
Works of the more ancient & consciously & profes-
sedly Inspired Men. will hold their proper rank. &
the Daughters of Memory shall become the Daugh-
ters of Inspiration. Shakspeare & Milton were
both curbd by the general malady & infection from
the silly Greek & Latin slaves of the Sword.—
Rouze up O Young Men of the New Age! set your
foreheads against the ignorant Hirelings! For
we have Hirelings in the Camp, the Court & the Uni-
versity; who would if they could, for ever depress Ment-
al & prolong Corporeal War; Painters! on you I call!
Sculptors! Architects! Suffer not the fashonable Fools
to depress your powers by the prices they pretend to
give for contemptible works or the expensive advert-
izing boasts that they make of such works; believe
Christ & his Apostles that there is a Class of Men
whose whole delight is in Destroying. We do not
want either Greek or Roman Models if we are but
just & true to our own Imaginations. those Worlds
of Eternity in which we shall live for ever; in
Jesus our Lord.

And did those feet in ancient time.
Walk upon Englands mountains green:
And was the holy Lamb of God.
On Englands pleasant pastures seen!

And did the Countenance Divine.
Shine forth upon our clouded hills?
And was Jerusalem builded here.
Among these dark Satanic Mills?

Bring me my Bow of burning gold:
Bring me my Arrows of desire:
Bring me my Spear: O clouds unfold!
Bring me my Chariot of fire!

I will not cease from Mental Fight.
Nor shall my Sword sleep in my hand:
Till we have built Jerusalem.
In Englands green & pleasant Land

Would to God that all the Lords people
were Prophets   Numbers XI ch 29 v

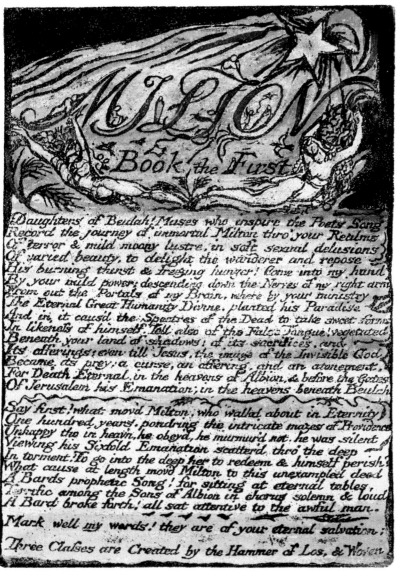

MILTON

Book the First

Daughters of Beulah! Muses who inspire the Poets Song
Record the journey of immortal Milton thro' your Realms
Of terror & mild moony lustre, in soft sexual delusions
Of varied beauty, to delight the wanderer and repose
His burning thirst & freezing hunger! Come into my hand
By your mild power; descending down the Nerves of my right arm
From out the Portals of my Brain, where by your ministry
The Eternal Great Humanity Divine. planted his Paradise,
And in it caus'd the Spectres of the Dead to take sweet forms
In likeness of himself. Tell also of the False Tongue! vegetated
Beneath your land of shadows: of its sacrifices. and
Its offerings; even till Jesus, the image of the Invisible God,
Became its prey; a curse, an offering, and an atonement,
For Death Eternal in the heavens of Albion, & before the Gates
Of Jerusalem his Emanation; in the heavens beneath Beulah

Say first! what mov'd Milton, who walld about in Eternity
One hundred years, pondring the intricate mazes of Providence
Unhappy tho in heav'n, he obeyd, he murmur'd not, he was silent
Viewing his Sixfold Emanation scatter'd thro' the deep
In torment! To go into the deep her to redeem & himself perish?
What cause at length mov'd Milton to this unexampled deed
A Bards prophetic Song! for sitting at eternal tables,
Terrific among the Sons of Albion in chorus solemn & loud,
A Bard broke forth! all sat attentive to the awful man.

Mark well my words! they are of your eternal salvation:

Three Classes are Created by the Hammer of Los, & Woven

From Golgonooza the spiritual Four-fold London eternal
In immense labours & sorrows, ever building, ever falling.
Thro Albions four Forests which overspread all the Earth,
From London Stone to Blackheath east: to Hounslow west:
To Finchley north; to Norwood south: and the weights
Of Enitharmons Loom play lulling cadences on the
    winds of Albion.
From Caithness in the north, to Lizard-point & Dover in the south

Loud sounds the Hammer of Los, & loud his Bellows is heard
Before London to Hampsteads breadths & Highgates heights To
Stratford & old Bow: & across to the Gardens of Kensington
On Tyburns Brook: loud groans Thames beneath the iron Forge
Of Rintrah & Palamabron of Theotorm & Bromion, to
    forge the instruments
Of Harvest: the Plow & Harrow to pass over the Nations

The Surrey hills glow like the clinkers of the furnace: Lambeths Vale
Where Jerusalems foundations began: where they were laid in ruins
Where they were laid in ruins from every Nation & Oak Groves rooted
Dark gleams before the Furnace-mouth, a heap of burning ashes
When shall Jerusalem return & overspread all the Nations
Return: return to Lambeths Vale O building of human souls
Thence stony Druid Temples overspread the Island white
And thence from Jerusalems ruins, from her walls of salvation
And praise: thro the whole Earth were reard from Ireland
To Mexico & Peru west, & east to China & Japan: till Babel
The Spectre of Albion frownd over the Nations in glory & war
All things begin & end in Albions ancient Druid rocky shore
But now the Starry Heavens are fled from the mighty limbs of
    Albion

Loud sounds the Hammer of Los, loud turn the Wheels of Enith-
Her Looms vibrate with soft affections, weaving the Web of Life
Out from the ashes of the Dead; Los lifts his iron Ladles
With molten ore: he heaves the iron cliffs in his rattling chains
From Hyde Park to the Alms-houses of Mile-end & old Bow
Here the Three Classes of Mortal Men take their fix'd destinations
And hence they overspread the Nations of the whole Earth & hence
The Web of Life is woven: & the tender sinews of life created
And the Three Classes of Men regulated by Los's Hammer, and
    woven

By Enitharmons Looms. & Spun beneath the Spindle of Tirzah
The first. The Elect from before the foundation of the World:
The second. The Redeemd. The Third. The Reprobate & form'd
To destruction from the mothers womb: follow with me my plow.

Of the first class was Satan: with incomparable mildness;
His primitive tyrannical attempts on Los: with most enduring love
He soft entreated Los to give to him Palamabrons station:
For Palamabron returnd with labour wearied every evening
Palamabron oft refus'd: and as often Satan offerd
His service till by repeated offers and repeated intreaties
Los gave to him the Harrow of the Almighty; alas blamable
Palamabron. feard to be ungry lest Satan should accuse him of
Ingratitude. & Los believe the accusation thro Satans extreme
Mildness. Satan labourd all day. it was a thousand years
In the evening returning terrified overlabourd & astonishd
Embrac'd soft with a brothers tears Palamabron. who also wept

Mark well my words, they are of your eternal salvation

Next morning Palamabron rose: the horses of the Harrow
Were maddend with tormenting fury, & the servants of the Harrow
The Gnomes, accus'd Satan. with indignation fury and fire.
Then Palamabron reddening like the Moon in an eclipse,
Spoke saying, You know Satans mildness and his self-imposition,
Seeming a brother, being a tyrant, even thinking himself a brother
While he is murdering the just: prophetic I behold
His future course thro' darkness and despair to eternal death
But we must not be tyrants also: he hath assum'd my place
For one whole day. under pretence of pity and love to me:
My horses hath he maddend! and my fellow servants injur'd:
How should he know the duties of another? O foolish forbearance
Would I had told Los. all my heart! but patience O my friends,
All may be well: silent remain, while I call Los and Satan.

Loud as the wind of Beulah that unroots the rocks & hills
Palamabron call'd! and Los & Satan came before him
And Palamabron shewd the horses, & the servants. Satan wept,
And mildly cursing Palamabron, him accus'd of crimes
Himself had wrought. Los trembled: Satans blandishments almost
Perswaded the Prophet of Eternity that Palamabron
Was Satans enemy, & that the Gnomes being Palamabrons friends
Were leagued together against Satan thro' ancient enmity.
What could Los do? how could he judge, when Satans self believd.
That he had not oppres'd the horses of the Harrow, nor the servants.

So Los said, Henceforth Palamabron, let each his own station
Keep: nor in pity false, nor in officious brotherhood, where
None needs, be active. Mean time Palamabrons horses.
Rag'd with thick flames redundant, & the Harrow maddend with fury.
Trembling Palamabron stood, the strongest of Demons trembled:
Curbing his living creatures; many of the strongest Gnomes.
They bit in their wild fury, who also maddend like wildest beasts

Mark well my words; they are of your eternal salvation

Mean while wept Satan before Los. accusing Palamabron
Himself exculpating with mildest speech. for himself believ'd
That he had not opress'd nor injur'd the refractory servants.

But Satan returning to his Mills (for Palamabron had serv'd
The Mills of Satan as the easier task) found all confusion;
And back return'd to Los. not fill'd with vengeance but with tears,
Himself convinc'd of Palamabrons turpitude. Los beheld
The servants of the Mills drunken with wine and dancing wild
With shouts and Palamabrons songs, rending the forests green
With echoing confusion. tho' the Sun was risen on high.

Then Los took off his left sandal placing it on his head.
Signal of solemn mourning: when the servants of the Mills
Beheld the signal they in silence stood. tho' drunk with wine
Los wept! But Rintrah also came, and Enitharmon on
His arm leand tremblingly observing all these things.

And Los said, Ye Genii of the Mills: the Sun is on high
Your labours call you. Palamabron is also in sad dilemma;
His horses are mad! his Harrow confounded! his companions enraged
Mine is the fault! I should have remember'd that pity divides the soul
And man, unmans: follow with me my Plow. this mournful day
Must be a blank in Nature: follow with me, and tomorrow again
Resume your labours, & this day shall be a mournful day

Wildly they follow'd Los and Rintrah, & the Mills were silent
They mourn'd all day this mournful day of Satan & Palamabron:
And all the Elect & all the Redeem'd mourn'd one toward another
Upon the mountains of Albion among the cliffs of the Dead.

They Plow'd in tears! incessant pour'd Jehovahs rain. & Molechs
thick fires contending with the rain, thunder'd above rolling
Terrible over their heads; Satan wept over Palamabron
Theotormon & Bromion contended on the side of Satan
Pitying his youth and beauty; trembling at eternal death:
Michael contended against Satan in the rolling thunder
Thulloh the friend of Satan also reprov'd him; faint their reproof.

But Rintrah who is of the reprobate: of those Form'd to destruction
In indignation. for Satans soft dissimulation of friendship!
Flam'd above all the plowed furrows, angry red and furious.
Till Michael sat down in the furrow weary dissolv'd in tears
Satan who drave the team beside him, stood angry & red
He smote Thulloh & slew him, & he stood terrible over Michael
Urging him to arise; he wept: Enitharmon saw his tears
But Los hid Thulloh from her sight, lest she should die of grief
She wept: she trembled! she kissed Satan; she wept over Michael
She formd a Space for Satan & Michael & for the poor infected
Trembling she wept over the Space, & closd it with a tender Moon

Los secret buried Thulloh. weeping disconsolate over the moony Space

But Palamabron called down a Great Solemn Assembly,
That he who will not defend Truth. may be compelled to
Defend a Lie. that he may be snared & caught & taken

And all Eden descended into Palamabrons tent
Among Albions Druids & Bards. in the caves beneath Albions
Death Couch. in the caverns of death. in the corner of the Atlantic.
And in the midst of the Great Assembly Palamabron prayd:
O God protect me from my friends. that they have not power over me
Thou hast givn me power to protect myself from my bitterest enemies.

Mark well my words, they are of your eternal salvation

Then rose the Two Witnesses, Rintrah & Palamabron:
And Palamabron appeald to all Eden, and recievd
Judgment: and Lo! it fell on Rintrah and his rage:
Which now flamd high & furious in Satan against Palamabron
Till it became a proverb in Eden. Satan is among the Reprobate.

Los in his wrath. cursd heaven & earth. he rent up Nations
Standing on Albions rocks among high-reard Druid temples
Which reach the stars of heaven & stretch from pole to pole.
He displacd continents, the oceans fled before his face
He alterd the poles of the world. east. west & north & south
But he closd up Enitharmon from the sight of all these things

For Satan flaming with Rintrahs fury hidden beneath his own mildness
Accusd Palamabron before the Assembly of ingratitude: of malice:
He created Seven deadly Sins drawing out his infernal scroll.
Of Moral laws and cruel punishments upon the clouds of Jehovah
To pervert the Divine voice in its entrance to the earth
With thunder of war & trumpets sound, with armies of disease
Punishments & deaths musterd & numberd; Saying I am God alone
There is no other! let all obey my principles of moral individuality
I have brought them from the uppermost innermost recesses
Of my Eternal Mind, transgressors I will rend off for ever,
As now I rend this accursed Family from my covering.

Thus Satan ragd amidst the Assembly! and his bosom grew
Opake against the Divine Vision; the paved terraces of
His bosom inwards shone with fires, but the stones becoming opake!
Hid him from sight. in an extreme blackness and darkness,
And there a World of deeper. Ulro was opend, in the midst
Of the Assembly. In Satans bosom a vast unfathomable Abyss.

Astonishment held the Assembly in an awful silence; and tears
Fell down as dews of night. & a loud solemn universal groan
Was utterd from the east & from the west & from the South
And from the north; and Satan stood opake immeasurable
Covering the east with solid blackness, round his hidden heart
With thunders utterd from his hidden wheels: accusing loud
The Divine Mercy. for protecting Palamabron in his tent.

Rintrah reard up walls of rocks and pourd rivers & moats
Of fire round the walls: columns of fire guard around
Between Satan and Palamabron in the terrible darkness.

And Satan not having the Science of Wrath. but only of Pity:
Rent them asunder. and wrath was left to wrath. & pity to pity.
He sunk down a dreadful Death, unlike the slumbers of Beulah

The Separation was terrible: the Dead was reposd on his Couch
Beneath the Couch of Albion. on the seven mountains of Rome
In the whole place of the Covering Cherub. Rome Babylon & Tyre.
His Spectre raging furious descended into its Space

He set his face against Jerusalem to destroy the Four of Albion

But Los hid Enitharmon from the sight of all these things
Upon the Thames whose lulling harmony reposd her soul:
Where Beulah lovely terminates in rocky Albion:
Terminating in Hyde Park. on Tyburns awful brook.

And the Mills of Satan were separated into a moony Space
Among the rocks of Albions Temples. and Satans Druid sons
Offer the Human Victims throughout all the Earth and Albions
Dread Tomb immortal on his Rock. overshadowd the whole Earth:
Where Satan making to himself Laws from his own identity.
Compelld others to serve him in moral gratitude & submission
Being calld God: setting himself above all that is called God
And all the Spectres of the Dead calling themselves Sons of God
In his Synagogues worship Satan under the Unutterable Name

And it was enquird: Why in a Great Solemn Assembly
The Innocent should be condemnd for the Guilty? Then an Eternal rose

Saying. If the Guilty should be condemnd he must be an Eternal Death
And one must die for another throughout all Eternity.
Satan is falln from his station & never can be redeemd
But must be new Created continually moment by moment
And therefore the Class of Satan shall be calld the Elect, & those
Of Rintrah. the Reprobate. & those of Palamabron the Redeemd
For he is redeemd from Satans Law, the wrath falling on Rintrah
And therefore Palamabron dared not to call a solemn Assembly
Till Satan had assumd Rintrahs wrath in the day of mourning
In a feminine delusion of false pride self-decievd.

So spoke the Eternal and confirmd it with a thunderous oath

But when Leutha (a Daughter of Beulah) beheld Satans condemna-
She down descended into the midst of the Great Solemn Assembly
Offering herself a Ransom for Satan, taking on her. his Sin

Mark well my words, they are of your eternal salvation:
                                                           -cing

And Leutha stood glowing with varying colours immortal, heart-pier
And lovely: & her moth-like elegance shone over the Assembly

At length standing upon the golden floor of Palamabron
She spoke: I am the Author of this Sin: by my suggestion
My Parent power Satan has committed this transgression
I loved Palamabron & I sought to approach his Tent,
But beautiful Elynittria with her silver arrows repelld me

For her light is terrible to me. I fade before her immortal beauty.
O, wherefore doth a Dragon-form forth issue from my limbs
To sieze her new born son! Ah me! the wretched Leutha!.
This to prevent, entering the doors of Satans brain night after night
Like sweet perfumes, I stupified the masculine perceptions
And kept only the feminine awake. hence rose his soft
Delusory love to Palamabron: admiration joind with envy
Cupidity unconquerable! my fault, when at noon of day
The Horses of Palamabron call'd for rest and pleasant death:
I sprang out of the breast of Satan, over the Harrow beaming
In all my beauty! that I might unloose the flaming steeds
As Elynittria used to do: but too well those living creatures
Knew that I was not Elynittria, and they brake the traces
But me, the servants of the Harrow saw not: but as a bow
Of varying colours on the hills; terribly rag'd the horses.
Satan astonish'd, and with power above his own controll
Compell'd the Gnomes to curb the horses, & to throw banks of sand
Around the fiery flaming Harrow in labyrinthine forms.
And brooks between to intersect the meadows in their course.
The Harrow cast thick flames: Jehovah thunder'd above!
Chaos & ancient night fled from beneath the fiery Harrow:
The Harrow cast thick flames & orbil us round in concave fires
A Hell of our own making, see, its flames still gird me round
Jehovah thunder'd above! Satan in pride of heart
Drove the fierce Harrow among the constellations of Jehovah
Drawing a third part in the fires as stubble north & south
To devour Albion and Jerusalem the Emanation of Albion
Driving the Harrow in Pitys paths. 'twas then with our dark fires
Which now gird round us (O eternal torment) I form'd the Serpent
Of precious stones & gold turn'd poisons on the sultry wastes
The Gnomes in all that day spar'd not: they cursed Satan bitterly.
To do unkind things in kindness! with power arm'd, to say
The most irritating things in the midst of tears and love
These are the stings of the Serpent! thus did we by them; till thus
They in return retaliated, and the Living Creatures madden'd.
The Gnomes labour'd. I weeping hid in Satans inmost brain:
But when the Gnomes refus'd to labour more, with blandishments
I came forth from the head of Satan: back the Gnomes recoil'd.
And call'd me Sin, and for a sign portentous held me. Soon
Day sunk and Palamabron return'd, trembling I hid myself
In Satans inmost Palace of his nervous fine wrought Brain:
For Elynittria met Satan with all her singing women.
Terrific in their joy & pouring wine of wildest power
They gave Satan their wine: indignant at the burning wrath.
Wild with prophetic fury his former life became like a dream
Cloth'd in the Serpents folds, in selfish holiness demanding purity
Being most impure, self-condemn'd to eternal tears, he drove
Me from his inmost Brain & the doors clos'd with thunders sound
O Divine Vision who didst create the Female: to repose
The Sleepers of Beulah; pity the repentant Leutha, My

Sick Couch bears the dark shades of Eternal Death infolding
The Spectre of Satan. he furious refuses to repose in sleep
I humbly bow in all my Sin before the Throne Divine,
Not so the Sick-one; Alas what shall be done him to restore,
Who calls the Individual Law, Holy; and despises the Saviour.
Glorying to involve Albions Body in fires of eternal War —

Now Leutha ceasd: tears flowd: but the Divine Pity supported her.
All is my fault! We are the Spectre, of Luvah the murderer
Of Albion: O Vala! O Luvah! O Albion! O lovely Jerusalem
The Sin was begun in Eternity, and will not rest to Eternity
Till two Eternitys meet together, Ah! lost! lost! lost! for ever!

So Leutha spoke. But when she saw that Enitharmon had
Created a New Space to protect Satan from punishment;
She fled to Enitharmons Tent & hid herself. Loud raging
Thunderd the Assembly dark & clouded. and they ratify'd
The kind decision of Enitharmon & gave a Time to the Space,
Even Six Thousand years; and sent Lucifer for its Guard.
But Lucifer refus'd to die & in pride he forsook his charge
And they elected Molech, and when Molech was impatient
The Divine hand found the Two Limits: first of Opacy, then of Contraction
Opacity was named Satan, Contraction was named Adam
Triple Elohim came: Elohim wearied fainted: they elected Shaddai.
Shaddai angry, Pahad descended: Pahad terrified, they sent Jehovah
And Jehovah was leprous; loud he calld, stretching his hand to Eternity
For then the Body of Death was perfected in hypocritic holiness.
Around the Lamb, a Female Tabernacle woven in Cathedrons Looms
He died as a Reprobate. he was Punish'd as a Transgressor!
Glory! Glory! Glory! to the Holy Lamb of God
I touch the heavens as an instrument to glorify the Lord!

The Elect shall meet the Redeem'd, on Albions rocks they shall meet
Astonish'd at the Transgressor, in him beholding the Saviour.
And the Elect shall say to the Redeemd. We behold it is of Divine
Mercy alone! of Free Gift and Election that we live.
Our Virtues & Cruel Goodnesses, have deserv'd Eternal Death.
Thus they weep upon the fatal Brook of Albions River.

But Elynittria met Leutha in the place where she was hidden.
And threw aside her arrows. and laid down her sounding Bow.
She soothd her with soft words & brought her to Palamabrons bed
In moments new created for delusion inter-woven round about.
In dreams she bore the shadowy Spectre of Sleep, & namd him Death.
In dreams she bore Rahab the mother of Tirzah & her sisters.
In Lambeths vales; in Cambridge & in Oxford, places of Thought
Intricate labyrinths of Times and Spaces unknown, that Leutha lived
In Palamabrons Tent. and Oothoon was her charming guard.

The Bard ceas'd. All consider'd and a loud resounding murmur
Continud round the Halls; and much they questiond the immortal
Loud voicd Bard. and many condemnd the high toned Song
Saying Pity and Love are too venerable for the imputation
Of Guilt. Others said. If it is true! if the acts have been performd
Let the Bard himself witness. Where hadst thou this terrible Song

The Bard replied. I am Inspired! I know it is Truth! for I Sing

According to the inspiration of the Poetic Genius
Who is the eternal all-protecting Divine Humanity
To whom be Glory & Power & Dominion Evermore Amen

Then there was great murmuring in the Heavens of Albion
Concerning Generation & the Vegetative power & concerning
The Lamb the Saviour: Albion trembled to Italy Greece & Egypt
To Tartary & Hindostan & China & to Great America
Shaking the roots & fast foundations of the Earth in doubtfulness
The loud voicd Bard terrifyd took refuge in Miltons bosom

Then Milton rose up from the heavens of Albion ardorous!
The whole Assembly wept prophetic, seeing in Miltons face
And in his lineaments divine the shades of Death & Ulro
He took off the robe of the promise, & ungirded himself from
the oath of God

And Milton said, I go to Eternal Death! The Nations still
Follow after the detestable Gods of Priam: in pomp
Of warlike selfhood. contradicting and blaspheming.
When will the Resurrection come; to deliver the sleeping body
From corruptibility; O when Lord Jesus wilt thou come?
Tarry no longer; for my soul lies at the gates of death.
I will arise and look forth for the morning of the grave.
I will go down to the sepulcher to see if morning breaks!
I will go down to self annihilation and eternal death,
Lest the Last Judgment come & find me unannihilate
And I be siezd & givin into the hands of my own Selfhood
The Lamb of God is seen thro' mists & shadows, hovring
Over the sepulchers in clouds of Jehovah & winds of Elohim
A disk of blood, distant; & heavns & earths roll dark between
What do I here before the Judgment? without my Emanation?
With the daughters of memory, & not with the daughters of inspiration
I in my Selfhood am that Satan: I am that Evil One!
He is my Spectre! in my obedience to loose him from my Hells
To claim the Hells, my Furnaces, I go to Eternal Death.

And Milton said, I go to Eternal Death; Eternity shudderd
For he took the outside course, among the graves of the dead
A mournful shade, Eternity shudderd at the image of eternal death

Then on the verge of Beulah he beheld his own Shadow;
A mournful form double; hermaphroditic: male & female
In one wonderful body, and he enterd into it
In direful pain for the dread shadow, twenty-seven fold
Reachd to the depths of direst Hell, & thence to Albions land:
Which is this earth of vegetation on which now I write.

The Seven Angels of the Presence wept over Miltons Shadow;

As when a man dreams, he reflects not that his body sleeps,
Else he would wake; so seemd he entering his Shadow: but
With him the Spirits of the Seven Angels of the Presence
Entering; they gave him still perceptions of his Sleeping Body;
Which now arose and walkd with them in Eden, as an Eighth
Image Divine tho' darkend; and tho walking as one walks
In sleep; and the Seven comforted and supported him.

Like as a Polypus that vegetates beneath the deep:
They saw his Shadow vegetated underneath the Couch
Of death: for when he enterd into his Shadow: Himself:
His real and immortal Self; was as appeard to those
Who dwell in immortality, as One sleeping on a couch
Of gold; and those in immortality gave forth their Emanations
Like Females of sweet beauty, to guard round him & to feed
His lips with food of Eden in his cold and dim repose!
But to himself he seemd a wanderer lost in dreary night.

Onwards his Shadow kept its course among the Spectres; calld
Satan, but swift as lightning passing them, startled the shades
Of Hell beheld him in a trail of light as of a comet
That travels into Chaos: so Milton went guarded within.

The nature of infinity is this! That every thing has its
Own Vortex; and when once a traveller thro' Eternity.
Has passd that Vortex, he percieves it roll backward behind
His path, into a globe itself infolding; like a sun:
Or like a moon, or like a universe of starry majesty.
While he keeps onwards in his wondrous journey on the earth
Or like a human form, a friend with whom he livd benevolent.
As the eye of man views both the east & west encompassing
Its vortex; and the north & south, with all their starry host;
Also the rising sun & setting moon he views surrounding
His corn-fields and his valleys of five hundred acres square.
Thus is the earth one infinite plane, and not as apparent
To the weak traveller confind beneath the moony shade.
Thus is the heaven a vortex passd already, and the earth
A vortex not yet passd by the traveller thro' Eternity.

First Milton saw Albion upon the Rock of Ages,
Deadly pale outstretchd and snowy cold, storm coverd;
A Giant form of perfect beauty, outstretchd on the rock
In solemn death; the Sea of Time & Space thunderd aloud
Against the rock, which was inwrapped with the weeds of death
Hovering over the cold bosom, in its vortex Milton bent down
To the bosom of death, what was underneath soon seemd above.
A cloudy heaven mingled with stormy seas in loudest ruin;
But as a wintry globe descends precipitant thro' Beulah bursting,
With thunders loud and terrible: so Miltons shadow fell,
Precipitant loud thundring into the Sea of Time & Space.

Then first I saw him in the Zenith as a falling star,
Descending perpendicular, swift as the swallow or swift;
And on my left foot falling on the tarsus, enterd there:
But from my left foot a black cloud redounding spread over Europe.

Then Milton knew that the Three Heavens of Beulah were beheld
By him on earth in his bright pilgrimage of sixty years

To Annihilate the Self-hood of Deceit &
False Forgivenefs

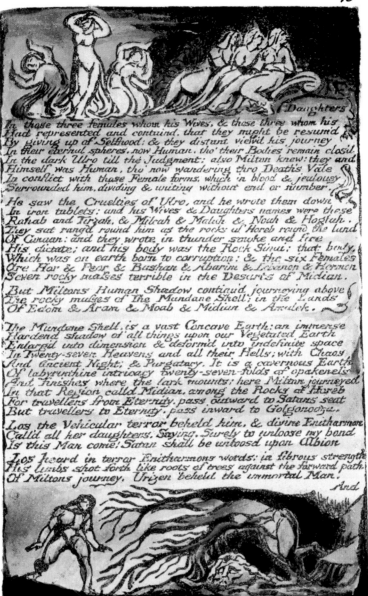

Daughters

In those three females whom his Wives, & these three whom his
Had represented and contain'd, that they might be resum'd
By giving up of Selfhood: & they distant view'd his journey
In their eternal spheres. now Human. tho' their Bodies remain clos'd
In the dark Ulro till the Judgment: also Milton knew: they and
Himself was Human. tho' now wandering thro Death's Vale
In conflict with those Female forms, which in blood & jealousy
Surrounded him, dividing & uniting without end or number.

He saw the Cruelties of Ulro, and he wrote them down
In iron tablets: and his Wives & Daughters names were these
Rahab and Tirzah, & Milcah & Malah & Noah & Hoglah.
They sat rang'd round him as the rocks of Horeb round the land
Of Canaan: and they wrote in thunder smoke and fire
His dictate; and his body was the Rock Sinai: that body,
Which was on earth born to corruption: & the six Females
Are Hor & Peor & Bashan & Abarim & Lebanon & Hermon
Seven rocky masses terrible in the Deserts of Midian.

But Miltons Human Shadow continu'd journeying above
The rocky masses of The Mundane Shell; in the Lands
Of Edom & Aram & Moab & Midian & Amalek.

The Mundane Shell, is a vast Concave Earth: an immense
Harden'd shadow of all things upon our Vegetated Earth
Enlarg'd into dimension & deform'd into indefinite space
In Twenty-seven Heavens and all their Hells; with Chaos
And Ancient Night; & Purgatory. It is a cavernous Earth
Of labyrinthine intricacy twenty-seven-folds of opakeness
And finishes where the lark mounts; here Milton journeyed
In that Region call'd Midian, among the Rocks of Horeb
For travellers from Eternity. pass outward to Satans seat,
But travellers to Eternity. pass inward to Golgonooza.

Los the Vehicular terror beheld him, & divine Enitharmon
Call'd all her daughters, Saying. Surely to unloose my bond
Is this Man come! Satan shall be untoosd upon Albion

Los heard in terror Enitharmons words: in fibrous strength
His limbs shot forth like roots of trees against the forward path
Of Miltons journey. Urizen beheld the immortal Man.

And

And he also darkend his brows: freezing dark rocks between
The footsteps. and infixing deep the feet in marble beds:
That Milton labourd with his journey. & his feet bled sore
Upon the clay now changd to marble: also Urizen rose.
And met him on the shores of Arnon: & by the streams of the brooks

Silent they met. and silent strove among the streams of Arnon
Even to Mahanaim. when with cold hand Urizen stoop'd down
And took up water from the river Jordan: pouring on
To Miltons brain the icy fluid from his broad cold palm.
But Milton took of the red clay of Succoth. moulding it with care
Between his palms: and filling up the furrows of many years
Beginning at the feet of Urizen. and on the bones
Creating new flesh on the Demon cold. and building him.
As with new clay a Human form in the Valley of Beth Peor.

Four Universes round the Mundane Egg remain Chaotic
One to the North. named Urthona: One to the South. named Urizen:
One to the East. named Luvah: One to the West. named Tharmas
They are the Four Zoa's that stood. around the Throne Divine:
But when Luvah assum'd the World of Urizen to the South:
And Albion was slain upon his mountains. & in his tent:
All fell towards the Center in dire ruin. sinking down.
And in the South remains a burning fire: in the East a void.
In the West, a world of raging waters: in the North a solid.
Unfathomable! without end. But in the midst of these,
Is built eternally the Universe of Los and Enitharmon:
Towards which Milton went. but Urizen oppos'd his path.

The Man and Demon strove many periods. Rahab beheld
Standing on Carmel: Rahab and Tirzah trembled to behold
The enormous strife. one giving life. the other giving death
To his adversary. and they sent forth all their sons & daughters
In all their beauty to entice Milton across the river.

The Twofold form Hermaphroditic: and the Double-sexed:
The Female-male, & the Male-female, self-dividing stood
Before him in their beauty, & in cruelties of holiness:
Shining in darkness. glorious upon the deeps of Entuthon.

Saying. Come thou to Ephraim! behold the Kings of Canaan!
The beautiful Amalekites, behold the fires of youth
Bound with the Chain of Jealousy by Los & Enitharmon:
The banks of Cam: cold learnings streams: Londons darkfrowning towers:
Lament upon the winds of Europe in Rephaims Vale.
Because Ahania rent apart into a desolate night
Laments! & Enion wanders like a weeping inarticulate voice
And Vala labours for her bread & water among the Furnaces
Therefore bright Tirzah triumphs: putting on all beauty.
And all perfection. in her cruel sports among the Victims.
Come bring with thee Jerusalem with songs on the Grecian Lyre!
In Natural Religion: in experiments on Men.
Let her be Offerd up to Holiness! Tirzah numbers her:
She numbers with her fingers every fibre ere it grow:
Where is the Lamb of God? where is the promise of his coming?
Her shadowy Sisters form the bones. even the bones of Horeb:
Around the marrow: and the orbed scull around the brain:
His Images are born for War! for Sacrifice to Tirzah:
To Natural Religion! to Tirzah the Daughter of Rahab the Holy!
She ties the knot of nervous fibres, into a white brain!
She ties the knot of bloody veins, into a red hot heart!
Within her bosom Albion lies embalmd. never to awake
Hand is become a rock! Sinai & Horeb. is Hyle & Coban:
Scofeld is bound in iron armour before Reubens Gate:
She ties the knot of milky seed into two lovely Heavens.

Two yet but one; each in the other sweet reflected! these
Are our Three Heavens beneath the shades of Beulah, land of rest!
Come then to Ephraim & Manasseh O beloved-one!
Come to my ivory palaces O beloved of thy mother!
And let us bind thee in the bands of War & be thou King
Of Canaan and reign in Hazor where the Twelve Tribes meet.

So spoke they as in one voice! Silent Milton stood before
The darkend Urizen; as the sculptor silent stands before
His forming image; he walks round it patient labouring.
Thus Milton stood forming bright Urizen, while his Mortal part
Sat frozen in the rock of Horeb: and his Redeemed portion
Thus formd the Clay of Urizen; but within that portion
His real Human walkd above in power and majesty
Tho darkend; and the Seven Angels of the Presence attended him.

O how can I with my gross tongue that cleaveth to the dust,
Tell of the Fourfold Man, in starry numbers fitly orderd
Or how can I with my cold hand of clay! But thou O Lord
Do with me as thou wilt! for I am nothing, and vanity.
If thou chuse to elect a worm, it shall remove the mountains.
For that portion namd the Elect: the Spectrous body of Milton:
Redounding from my left foot into Los's Mundane space
Brooded over his Body in Horeb against the Resurrection
Preparing it for the Great Consummation; red the Cherub on Sinai
Glowd; but in terrors folded round his clouds of blood.

Now Albions sleeping Humanity began to turn upon his Couch;
Feeling the electric flame of Miltons awful precipitate descent.
Seest thou the little winged fly, smaller than a grain of sand?
It has a heart like thee; a brain open to heaven & hell,
Withinside wondrous & expansive; its gates are not closd,
I hope thine are not: hence it clothes itself in rich array;
Hence thou art clothd with human beauty O thou mortal man.
Seek not thy heavenly father then beyond the skies:
There Chaos dwells & ancient Night & Og & Anak old:
For every human heart has gates of brass & bars of adamant,
Which few dare unbar because dread Og & Anak guard the gates
Terrific! and each mortal brain is walld and moated round
Within: and Og & Anak watch here; here is the Seat
Of Satan in its Webs; for in brain and heart and loins
Gates open behind Satans Seat to the City of Golgonooza
Which is the spiritual fourfold London, in the loins of Albion

Thus Milton fell thro Albions heart, travelling outside of Humanity
Beyond the Stars in Chaos in Caverns of the Mundane Shell.

But many of the Eternals rose up from eternal tables
Drunk with the Spirit, burning round the Couch of death they stood
Looking down into Beulah: wrathful, filld with rage!
They rend the heavens round the Watchers in a fiery circle:
And round the Shadowy Eighth: the Eight close up the Couch
Into a tabernacle, and flee with cries down to the Deeps:
Where Los opens his three wide gates, surrounded by raging fires!
They soon find their own place & join the Watchers of the Ulro.

Los saw them and a cold pale horror coverd oer his limbs
Pondering he knew that Rintrah & Palamabron might depart:
Even as Reuben & as Gad; gave up himself to tears.
He sat down on his anvil-stock; and leand upon the trough,
Looking into the black water, mingling it with tears.

At last when desperation almost tore his heart in twain
He recollected an old Prophecy in Eden recorded,
And often sung to the loud harp at the immortal feasts
That Milton of the Land of Albion should up ascend
Forwards from Ulro from the Vale of Felpham; and set free
Orc from his Chain of Jealousy, he started at the thought

A3

And down descended into Udan-Adan: it was night:
And Satan sat sleeping upon his Couch in Udan-Adan:
His Spectre slept, his Shadow woke; when one sleeps th'other wakes

But Milton entering my Foot; I saw in the nether
Regions of the Imagination; also all men on Earth
And all in Heaven, saw in the nether regions of the Imagination
In Ulro beneath Beulah, the vast breach of Miltons descent.
But I knew not that it was Milton, for man cannot know
What passes in his members till periods of Space & Time
Reveal the secrets of Eternity: for more extensive
Than any other earthly things, are Mans earthly lineaments.

And all this Vegetable World appeard on my left Foot,
As a bright sandal formd immortal of precious stones & gold:
I stooped down & bound it on to walk forward thro' Eternity.

There is in Eden a sweet River, of milk & liquid pearl,
Namd Ololon; on whose mild banks dwelt those who Milton drove
Down into Ulro: and they wept in long resounding song
For seven days of eternity, and the rivers living banks
The mountains waild! & every plant that grew, in solemn sighs lamented.

When Luvahs bulls each morning drag the sulphur Sun out of the Deep
Harnessd with starry harness black & shining kept by black slaves
That work all night at the starry harness. Strong and vigorous
They drag the unwilling Orb: at this time all the Family
Of Eden heard the lamentation, and Providence began,
But when the clarions of day sounded they drownd the lamentations
And when night came all was silent in Ololon: & all refusd to lament
In the still night fearing lest they should others molest.

Seven morning Los heard them, as the poor bird within the shell
Hears its impatient parent bird; and Enitharmon heard them:
But saw them not, for the blue Mundane Shell inclosd them in.

And they lamented that they had in wrath & fury & fire
Driven Milton into the Ulro; for now they knew too late
That it was Milton the Awakener: they had not heard the Bard,
Whose song called Milton to the attempt; and Los heard these laments.
He heard them call in prayer all the Divine Family;
And he beheld the Cloud of Milton stretching over Europe.

But all the Family Divine collected as Four Suns
In the Four Points of heaven East, West & North & South,
Enlarging and enlarging till their Disks approachd each other;
And when they touchd closed together Southward in One Sun
Over Ololon: and as One Man, who weeps over his brother
In a dark tomb, so all the Family Divine, wept over Ololon.

Saying. Milton goes to Eternal Death! so saying, they groand in spirit
And were troubled! and again the Divine Family groaned in spirit!

And Ololon said, Let us descend also, and let us give
Ourselves to death in Ulro among the Transgressors.
Is Virtue a Punisher? O no! how is this wondrous thing?
This World beneath, unseen before; this refuge from the wars
Of Great Eternity! unnatural refuge! unknown by us till now!
Or are these the pangs of repentance! let us enter into them

Then the Divine Family said, Six Thousand Years are now
Accomplishd in this World of Sorrow; Miltons Angel knew
The Universal Dictate: and you also feel this Dictate.
And now you know this World of Sorrow, and feel Pity. Obey
The Dictate! Watch over this World, and with your brooding wings,
Renew it to Eternal Life: Lo! I am with you alway
But you cannot renew Milton he goes to Eternal Death

So spake the Family Divine as One Man even Jesus
Uniting in One with Ololon & the appearance of One Man
Jesus the Saviour appeard coming in the Clouds of Ololon:

Tho driven away with the Seven Starry Ones into the Ulro
Yet the Divine Vision remains Every-where For-ever. Amen.
And Ololon lamented for Milton with a great lamentation.

While Los heard indistinct in fear, what time I bound my sandals
On; to walk forward thro' Eternity, Los descended to me:
And Los behind me stood; a terrible flaming Sun: just close
Behind my back; I turned round in terror, and behold.
Los stood in that fierce glowing fire; & he also stoop'd down
And bound my sandals on in Udan-Adan; trembling I stood
Exceedingly with fear & terror, standing in the Vale
Of Lambeth: but he kissed me and wishd me health.
And I became One Man with him arising in my strength:
Twas too late now to recede. Los had enterd into my soul:
His terrors now possesd me whole! I arose in fury & strength.

I am that Shadowy Prophet who Six Thousand Years ago
Fell from my station in the Eternal bosom. Six Thousand Years
Are finishd. I return! both Time & Space obey my will.
I in Six Thousand Years walk up and down: for not one Moment
Of Time is lost, nor one Event of Space unpermanent
But all remain: every fabric of Six Thousand Years
Remains permanent: tho' on the Earth where Satan
Fell, and was cut off all things vanish & are seen no more
They vanish not from me & mine, we guard them first & last
The generations of men run on in the tide of Time
But leave their destind lineaments permanent for ever & ever.
So spoke Los as we went along to his supreme abode.

Rintrah and Palamabron met us at the Gate of Golgonooza
Clouded with discontent, & brooding in their minds terrible things

They said. O Father most beloved! O merciful Parent!
Pitying and permitting evil, tho strong & mighty to destroy.
Whence is this Shadow terrible? wherefore dost thou refuse
To throw him into the Furnaces! knowest thou not that he
Will unchain Orc? & let loose Satan. Og. Sihon & Anak.
Upon the Body of Albion? for this he is come: behold it written
Upon his fibrous left Foot black: most dismal to our eyes
The Shadowy Female shudders thro' heaven in torment inexpressible:
And all the Daughters of Los prophetic wail: yet in deceit.
They weave a new Religion from new Jealousy of Theotormon!
Miltons Religion is the cause: there is no end to destruction!
Seeing the Churches at their Period in terror & despair:
Rahab created Voltaire: Tirzah created Rousseau;
Asserting the Self-righteousness against the Universal Saviour
Mocking the Confessors & Martyrs, claiming Self-righteousness;
With cruel Virtue: making War upon the Lambs Redeemed;
To perpetuate War & Glory, to perpetuate the Laws of Sin:
They perverted Swedenborgs Visions in Beulah & in Ulro:
To destroy Jerusalem as a Harlot & her Sons as Reprobates;
To raise up Mystery the Virgin Harlot Mother of War,
Babylon the Great, the Abomination of Desolation:
O Swedenborg! strongest of men, the Samson shorn by the Churches!
Shewing the Transgresors in Hell, the proud Warriors in Heaven:
Heaven as a Punisher & Hell as One under Punishment:
With Laws from Plato & his Greeks to renew the Trojan Gods,
In Albion: & to deny the value of the Saviours blood.
But then I raisd up Whitefield, Palamabron raisd up Westley,
And these are the cries of the Churches before the two Witnesses
Faith in God the dear Saviour who took on the likeness of men:
Becoming obedient to death, even the death of the Cross
The Witnesses lie dead in the Street of the Great City
No Faith is in all the Earth: the Book of God is trodden under Foot:
He sent his two Servants Whitefield & Westley: were they Prophets
Or were they Idiots or Madmen? shew us Miracles!

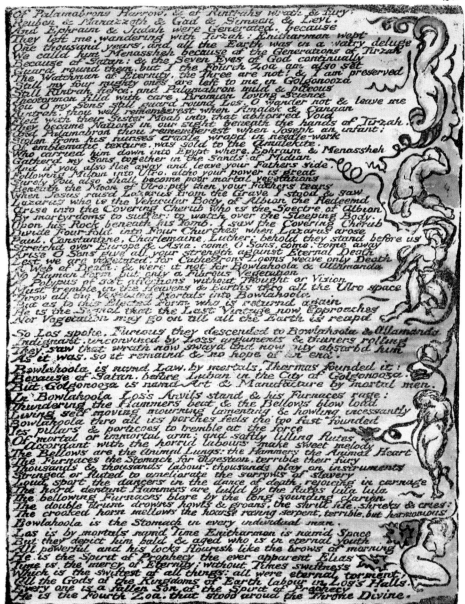

Of Palamabrons Harrow, & of Rintrahs wrath & fury:
Reuben & Manazzoth & Gad & Simeon & Levi,
And Ephraim & Judah were Generated. because
They left me. wandering with Tirzah: Enitharmon wept
One thousand years, and all the Earth was in a watry deluge
We called him Menassheh because of the Generations of Tirzah
Because of Satan: & the Seven Eyes of God continually
Guard round them. but I the Fourth Zoa am also set
The Watchman of Eternity, the Three are not! & I am preserved
Still Rintrah fierce, and Palamabron mild & pityous
They labour for me in Golgonooza
Decotarman stild with care. Bromion loving Science
You O my Sons still guard round Los, O wander not & leave me
Rintrah. thou well rememberest when Amalek & Canaan
Fled with their Sister Moab into that abhorred Void
They became Nations in our sight beneath the hands of Tirzah.
And Palamabron thou rememberest when Joseph an infant:
Stolen from his nurses cradle wrapd in needle-work
Of emblematic texture, was sold to the Amalekite,
Who carried him down into Egypt where, Ephraim & Menassheh
Gatherd my Sons together in the Sands of Midian
And if you also flee away and leave your Fathers side,
Following Milton into Ulro, altho your power is great
Surely you also shall become poor mortal vegetations
Beneath the Moon of Ulro: pity then your Fathers tears
When Jesus raisd Lazarus from the Grave I stood & saw
Lazarus who is the Vehicular Body of Albion the Redeemd
Arise into the Covering Cherub who is the Spectre of Albion
By martyrdoms to suffer: to watch over the Sleeping Body.
Upon his Rock beneath his Tomb. I saw the Covering Cherub
Divide Four-fold into Four Churches when Lazarus arose
Paul, Constantine, Charlemaine, Luther; behold they stand before us
Stretchd over Europe & Asia. come O Sons, come, come away
Arise O Sons give all your strength against Eternal Death
Lest we are vegetated for Cathedrons Looms weave only Death
A Web of Death: & were it not for Bowlahoola & Allamanda
No Human Form but only a Fibrous Vegetation
A Polypus of soft affections without Thought or Vision
Must tremble in the Heavens & Earths thro all the Ulro space
Throw all the Vegetated Mortals into Bowlahoola
But as to this Elected Form who is returnd again
He is the Signal that the Last Vintage now approaches
Nor Vegetation may go on till all the Earth is reapd

So Los spoke. Furious they descended to Bowlahoola & Allamanda
Indignant. unconvinced by Loss arguments & thunders rolling
They saw that wrath now swayd and now pity absorbd him
As it was, so it remaind & no hope of an end.

Bowlahoola is namd Law. by mortals, Thermas founded it:
Because of Satan. before Luban in the City of Golgonooza.
But Golgonooza is namd Art & Manufacture by mortal men.

In Bowlahoola Loss Anvils stand & his Furnaces rage:
Thundering the Hammers beat & the Bellows blow loud
Living self moving mourning lamenting & howling incessantly
Bowlahoola thro all its porches feels the too fast founded
Its pillars & porticoes to tremble at the force
Of mortal or immortal arm: and softly lilling flutes
Accordant with the horrid labours make sweet melody
The Bellows are the Animal Lungs: the Hammers the Animal Heart
The Furnaces the Stomach for digestion. terrible their fury
Thousands & thousands labour: thousands play on instruments
Stringed or fluted to ameliorate the sorrows of slavery
Loud sport the dancers in the dance of death, rejoicing in carnage
The hard dentant Hammers are lulld by the flutes lula lula
The bellowing Furnaces blare by the long sounding clarion
The double drum drowns howls & groans. the shrill fife. shrieks & cries:
The crooked horn mellows the hoarse raving serpent, terrible. but harmonious
Bowlahoola is the Stomach in every individual man.

Los is by mortals namd Time Enitharmon is namd Space
But they depict him bald & aged who is in eternal youth
All powerful and his locks flourish like the brows of morning
He is the Spirit of Prophecy the ever apparent Elias
Time is the mercy of Eternity; without Times swiftness
Which is the swiftest of all things: all were eternal torment:
All the Gods of the Kingdoms of Earth labour in Loss Halls.
Every one is a fallen Son of the Spirit of Prophecy
He is the Fourth Zoa. that stood aroud the Throne Divine.

But the Wine-press of Los is eastward of Golgonooza, before the Seat
Of Satan. Luvah laid the foundation & Urizen finishd it in howling woe.
How red the sons & daughters of Luvah: here they tread the grapes.
Laughing & shouting drunk with odours many fall, oerwearied
Drownd in the wine is many a youth & maiden: those around
Lay them on skins of Tygers & of the spotted Leopard & the Wild Ass
Till they revive, or bury them in cool grots, making lamentation.

This Wine-press is calld War on Earth, it is the Printing-Press
Of Los: and here he lays his words in order above the mortal brain
As cogs are formd in a wheel to turn the cogs of the adverse wheel.

Timbrels & violins sport round the Wine-presses: the little Seed;
The sportive Root, the Earth-worm, the gold Beetle: the wise Emmet;
Dance round the Wine-presses of Luvah: the Centipede is there:
The ground Spider with many eyes: the Mole clothed in velvet
The ambitious Spider in his sullen web; the lucky golden Spinner;
The Earwig armd: the tender Maggot emblem of immortality:
The Flea: Louse: Bug: the Tape-Worm: all the Armies of Disease:
Visible or invisible to the slothful vegetating Man.
The slow Slug: the Grasshopper that sings & laughs & drinks:
Winter comes, he folds his slender bones without a murmur.
The cruel Scorpion is there: the Gnat: Wasp: Hornet & the Honey Bee:
The Toad & venomous Newt; the Serpent clothd in gems & gold:
They throw off their gorgeous raiment: they rejoice with loud jubilee
Around the Wine-presses of Luvah, naked & drunk with wine.

There is the Nettle that stings with soft down: and there
The indignant Thistle: whose bitterness is bred in his milk:
Who feeds on contempt of his neighbour: there all the idle Weeds
That creep around the obscure places, shew their various limbs:
Naked in all their beauty dancing round the Wine-presses.

But in the Wine-presses the Human grapes sing not, nor dance
They howl & writhe in shoals of torment; in fierce flames consuming,
In chains of iron & in dungeons circled with ceaseless fires.
In pits & dens & shades of death: in shapes of torment & woe.
The plates & screws & wracks & saws & cords & fires & cisterns
The cruel joys of Luvahs Daughters lacerating with knives
And whips their Victims & the deadly sport of Luvahs Sons.

They dance around the dying, & they drink the howl & groan
They catch the shrieks in cups of gold, they hand them to one another
These are the sports of love, & these the sweet delights of amorous play
Tears of the grape, the death sweat of the cluster the last sigh
Of the mild youth who listens to the lureing songs of Luvah.

But Allamanda calld on Earth Commerce, is the Cultivated land
Around the City of Golgonooza in the Forests of Entuthon:
Here the Sons of Los labour against Death Eternal; through all
The Twenty-seven Heavens of Beulah in Ulro, Seat of Satan:
Which is the False Tongue beneath Beulah: it is the Sense of Touch:
The Plow goes forth in tempests & lightnings & the Harrow cruel
In blights of the east; the heavy Roller follows in howlings of woe.

Urizens sons here labour also; & here are seen the Mills
Of Theotormon, on the verge of the Lake of Udan-Adan:
These are the starry voids of night & the depths & caverns of earth
These Mills are oceans, clouds & waters ungovernable in their fury;
Here are the stars created & the seeds of all things planted
And here the Sun & Moon recieve their fixed destinations.

But in Eternity the Four Arts: Poetry, Painting, Music,
And Architecture which is Science: are the Four Faces of Man.
Not so in Time & Space: there Three are shut out, and only
Science remains thro Mercy: & by means of Science, the Three
Became apparent in Time & Space, in the Three Professions

That Man may live upon Earth till the time of his awaking,
And from these Three, Science derives every Occupation of Men.
And Science is divided into Bowlahoola & Allamanda.

Loud shout the Sons of Luvah, at the Wine-presses as Los descended,
With Rintrah & Palamabron in his fires of resistless fury.
The Wine-press on the Rhine groans loud, but all its central beams
Act more terrific in the central Cities of the Nations
Where Human Thought is crushd beneath the iron hand of Power.
There Los puts all into the Press, the Opressor & the Opressed
Together, ripe for the Harvest & Vintage & ready for the Loom,

They sang at the Vintage. This is the Last Vintage! & Seed
Shall no more be sown upon Earth, till all the Vintage is over
And all gatherd in, till the Plow has pass'd over the Nations
And the Harrow & heavy thundering Roller upon the mountains

And loud the Souls howl round the Porches of Golgonooza
Crying O God deliver us to the Heavens or to the Earths.
That we may preach righteousness & punish the sinner with death
But Los refused, till all the Vintage of Earth was gatherd in.

And Los stood & cried to the Labourers of the Vintage in voice of awe.

Fellow Labourers! The Great Vintage & Harvest is now upon Earth
The whole extent of the Globe is explored, Every scatterd Atom
Of Human Intellect now is flocking to the sound of the Trumpet
All the Wisdom which was hidden in caves & dens, from ancient
Time; is now sought out from Animal & Vegetable & Mineral
The Awakener is come, outstretchd over Europe: the Vision of God is
fulfilled
The Ancient Man upon the Rock of Albion Awakes,
He listens to the sounds of War astonish'd & ashamed:
He sees his Children mock at Faith and deny Providence
Therefore you must bind the Sheaves not by Nations or Families
You shall bind them in Three Classes; according to their Classes
So shall you bind them. Separating What has been Mixed
Since Men began to be Wove into Nations by Rahab & Tirzah
Since Albions Death & Satans Cutting off from our awful Fields
When under pretence to benevolence the Elect Subdud All
From the Foundation of the World. The Elect is one Class: You
Shall bind them separate: they cannot Believe in Eternal Life
Except by Miracle & a New Birth. The other two Classes;
The Reprobate who never cease to Believe, and the Redeem'd
Who live in doubts & fears perpetually tormented by the Elect
These you shall bind in a twin-bundle for the Consummation,
But the Elect must be saved fires of Eternal Death
To be formed into the Churches of Beulah that they destroy not the
Earth
For in every Nation & every Family the Three Classes are born
And in every Species of Earth, Metal, Tree, Fish, Bird & Beast.
We form the Mundane Egg, that Spectres coming by fury or amity
All is the same, & every one remains in his own energy
Go forth Reapers with rejoicing, you sowed in tears
But the time of your refreshing cometh, only a little moment
Still abstain from pleasure & rest in the labours of eternity
And you shall Reap the whole Earth, from Pole to Pole: from Sea to Sea
Beginning at Jerusalems Inner Court, Lambeth ruind and given
To the detestable Gods of Priam, to Apollo: and at the Asylum
Given to Hercules, who labour in Tirzahs Looms for bread
Who set Pleasure against Duty: who Create Olympic crowns
To make Learning a burden & the Work of the Holy Spirit: Strife.
The Thor & cruel Odin who first rear'd the Polar Caves
Lambeth mourns calling Jerusalem, she weeps & looks abroad
For the Lords coming, that Jerusalem may overspread all Nations
Crave not for the mortal & perishing delights, but leave them
To the weak, and pity the weak as your infant care: Break not
Forth in your wrath lest you also are Vegetated by Tirzah
Wait till the Judgement is past, till the Creation is consumed
And then rush forward with me into the glorious spiritual
Vegetation; the Supper of the Lamb & his Bride: and the
Awaking of Albion our friend and ancient companion.
So Los spoke. But lightnings of discontent broke on all sides round,
And murmurs of thunder rolling heavy long & loud over the mountains
While Los calld his Sons around him to the Harvest & the Vintage.

Thou seest the Constellations in the deep & wondrous Night
They rise in order and continue their immortal courses
Upon the mountains & in vales with harp & heavenly song
With flute & clarion; with cups & measures filld with foaming wine
Glittering the streams reflect the Vision of beatitude,
And the calm Ocean joys beneath & smooths his awful waves:
These

These are the Sons of Los, & these the Labourers of the Vintage
Thou seest the gorgeous clothed Flies that dance &sport in summer
Upon the sunny brooks & meadows: every one the dance
Knows in its intricate mazes of delight artful to weave:
Each one to sound his instruments of music in the dance,
To touch each other & recede; to cross & change & return
These are the Children of Los; thou seest the Trees on mountains
The wind blows heavy, loud they thunder thro' the darksom sky
Uttering prophecies & speaking instructive words to the sons
Of men: These are the Sons of Los! These the Visions of Eternity
But we see only as it were the hem of their garments
When with our vegetable eyes we view these wondrous Visions

There are Two Gates thro which all Souls descend. One Southward
From Dover Cliff to Lizard Point, the other toward the North
Caithness & rocky Durness, Pentland & John Groats House

The Souls descending to the Body, wail on the right hand
Of Los: & those deliverd from the Body, on the left hand
For Los against the east his force continually bends
Along the Valleys of Middlesex from Hounslow to Blackheath
Lest those Three Heavens of Beulah should the Creation destroy
And lest they should descend before the north & south Gates
Groaning with pity, he among the wailing Souls laments

And these the Labours of the Sons of Los in Allamanda,
And in the City of Golgonooza: & in Luban: & around
The Lake of Udan-Adan, in the Forests of Entuthon Benython
Where Souls incessant wail, being piteous Passions & Desires
With neither lineament nor form but like to watry clouds
The Passions & Desires descend upon the hungry winds
For such alone Sleepers remain meer passion & appetite;
The Sons of Los clothe them & feed & provide houses & fields
And every Generated Body in its inward form,
Is a garden of delight & a building of magnificence,
Built by the Sons of Los in Bowlahoola & Allamanda
And the herbs & flowers & furniture & beds & chambers
Continually woven in the Looms of Enitharmons Daughters
In bright Cathedrons golden Dome with care & love & tears
For the various Classes of Men are all markd out determinate
In Bowlahoola; & as the Spectres choose their affinities
So they are born on Earth, & every Class is determinate
But not by Natural but by Spiritual power alone. Because
The Natural power continually seeks & tends to Destruction
Ending in Death: which would of itself be Eternal Death
And all are Classd by Spiritual, & not by Natural power.

And every Natural Effect has a Spiritual Cause, and Not
A Natural: for a Natural Cause only seems, it is a Delusion
Of Ulro: & a ratio of the perishing Vegetable Memory.

36

Some Sons of Los surround the Passions with porches of iron & silver
Creating form & beauty around the dark regions of sorrow.
Giving to airy nothing a name and a habitation
Delightful: with bounds to the Infinite putting off the Indefinite
Into most holy forms of Thought: (such is the power of inspiration)
They labour incessant; with many tears & afflictions:
Creating the beautiful House for the piteous sufferer.

Others; Cabinets richly fabricate of gold & ivory;
For Doubts & fears unform'd & wretched & melancholy
The little weeping Spectre stands on the threshold of Death
Eternal; and sometimes two Spectres like lamps quivering
And often malignant they combat (heart-breaking sorrowful & piteous)
Antamon takes them into his beautiful flexible hands,
As the Sower takes the seed, or as the Artist his clay
Or fine wax, to mould artful a model for golden ornaments.
The soft hands of Antamon draw the indelible line:
Form immortal with golden pen; such as the Spectre admiring
Puts on the sweet form; then smiles Antamon bright thro his windows
The Daughters of beauty look up from their Loom & prepare.
The integument soft for its clothing with joy & delight.

But Theotormon & Sotha stand in the Gate of Luban anxious
Their numbers are seven million & seven thousand & seven hundred
They contend with the weak Spectres, they fabricate soothing forms
The Spectre refuses, he seeks cruelty, they create the crested Cock
Terrified the Spectre screams & rushes in fear into their Net
Of kindness & compassion & is born a weeping terror.
Or they create the Lion & Tyger in compassionate thunderings
Howling the Spectres flee: they take refuge in Human lineaments

The Sons of Ozoth within the Optic Nerve stand fiery glowing
And the number of his Sons is eight millions & eight.
They give delights to the man unknown; artificial riches
They give to scorn, & their posessors to trouble & sorrow & care,
Shutting the sun & moon & stars & trees, & clouds, & waters,
And hills, out from the Optic Nerve & hardening it into a bone
Opake, and like the black pebble on the enraged beach.
While the poor indigent is like the diamond which tho clothd
In rugged covering in the mine, is open all within
And in his hallowd center holds the heavens of bright eternity
Ozoth here builds walls of rocks against the surging sea
And timbers cramp'd with iron cramps bar in the joys of life
From all destruction in the Spectrous cunning or rage. He Creates
The speckled Newt; the Spider & Beetle, the Rat & Mouse,
The Badger & Fox: they worship before his feet in trembling fear.

But others of the Sons of Los build Moments & Minutes & Hours
And Days & Months & Years & Ages & Periods: wondrous buildings
And every Moment has a Couch of gold for soft repose,
(A Moment equals a pulsation of the artery)
And between every two Moments stands a Daughter of Beulah
To feed the Sleepers on their Couches with maternal care.
And every Minute has an azure Tent with silken Veils.
And every Hour has a bright golden Gate carved with skill.
And every Day & Night has Walls of brass & Gates of adamant,
Shining like precious stones, & ornamented with appropriate signs:
And every Month, a silver paved Terrace builded high:
And every Year, invulnerable Barriers with high Towers.
And every Age is Moated deep with Bridges of silver & gold:
And every Seven Ages is Incircled with a Flaming Fire.
Now Seven Ages is amounting to Two Hundred Years
Each has its Guard, each Moment Minute Hour Day Month & Year.
All are the work of Fairy hands of the Four Elements
The Guard are Angels of Providence on duty evermore
Every Time less than a pulsation of the artery
Is equal in its period & value to Six Thousand Years.

For

37

For in this Period the Poets Work is Done; and all the Great
Events of Time start forth & are concievd in such a Period
Within a Moment: a Pulsation of the Artery.

The Sky is an immortal Tent built by the Sons of Los
And every Space that a Man views around his dwelling-place:
Standing on his own roof, or in his garden on a mount
Of twentyfive cubits in height. such Space is his Universe:
And on its verge the Sun rises & sets. the Clouds bow
To meet the flat Earth & the Sea in such an orderd Space:
The Starry heavens reach no further but here bend and set
On all sides & the two Poles turn on their valves of gold:
And if he move his dwelling-place. his heavens also move.
Whereer he goes & all his neighbourhood bewail his loss:
Such are the Spaces called Earth & such its dimension.
As to that false appearance which appears to the reasoner.
As of a Globe rolling thro Voidness, it is a delusion of Ulro
The Microscope knows not of this nor the Telescope. they alter
The ratio of the Spectators Organs but leave Objects untouchd
For every Space larger than a red Globule of Mans blood.
Is visionary: and is created by the Hammer of Los
And every Space smaller than a Globule of Mans blood. opens
Into Eternity of which this vegetable Earth is but a shadow:
The red Globule is the unwearied Sun by Los created
To measure Time and Space to mortal Men. every morning.
Bowlahoola & Allamanda are placed on each side
Of that Pulsation & that Globule. terrible their power.

But Rintrah. & Palamabron govern over Day & Night
In Allamanda & Entuthon Benython where Souls wail:
Where Orc incessant howls burning in fires of Eternal Youth.
Within the vegetated mortal Nerves; for every Man born is joined
Within into One mighty Polypus. and this Polypus is Orc.

But in the Optic vegetative Nerves Sleep was transformed
To Death in old time by Satan the father of Sin & Death
And Satan is the Spectre of Orc & Orc is the generate Luvah

But in the Nerves of the Nostrils. Accident being Formed
Into Substance & Principle. by the cruelties of Demonstration
It became Opake & Indefinite: but the Divine Saviour.
Formed it into a Solid by Los's Mathematic power.
He named the Opake Satan: he named the Solid Adam.

And in the Nerves of the Ear. (for the Nerves of the Tongue are closed)
On Albions Rock Los stands creating the glorious Sun each morning
And when unwearied in the evening he creates the Moon
Death to delude, who all in terror at their splendor leaves
His prey while Los appoints, & Rintrah & Palamabron guide
The Souls clear from the Rock of Death. that Death himself may wake
In his appointed season when the ends of heaven meet.

Then Los conducts the Spirits to be Vegetated, into
Great Golgonooza, free from the four iron pillars of Satans Throne
Temperance. Prudence. Justice. Fortitude. the four pillars of tyranny
That Satans Watch-Fiends touch them not before they Vegetate.

But Enitharmon and her Daughters take the pleasant charge.
To give them to their lovely heavens till the Great Judgment Day
Such is their lovely charge. But Rahab & Tirzah pervert
Their mild influences, therefore the Seven Eyes of God walk round
The Three Heavens of Ulro, where Tirzah & her Sisters
Weave the black Woof of Death upon Entuthon Benython
In the Vale of Surrey where Horeb terminates in Rephaim. The gore
The stamping feet of Zelophehads Daughters are coverd with Human
Upon the treddles of the Loom, they sing to the winged shuttle:
The River rises above his banks to wash the Woof:
He takes it in his arms: he pulses it in strength thro his current
The veil of human miseries is woven over the Ocean
From the Atlantic to the Great South Sea. the Erythrean.

Such is the World of Los the labour of six thousand years.
Thus Nature is a Vision of the Science of the Elohim.

                End of the First Book

How wide the Gulf & Unpassable! between Simplicity & Insipidity

Milton.

Contraries are Positives
A Negation is not a Contrary

Book the Second.

There is a place where Contrarieties are equally True
This place is called Beulah. It is a pleasant lovely Shadow
Where no dispute can come. Because of those who Sleep.
Into this place the Sons & Daughters of Ololon descended
With solemn mourning into Beulahs moony shades & hills
Weeping for Milton; mute wonder held the Daughters of Beulah
Entranced with affection sweet and mild & holy love.

Beulah is ev'ry more Created around Eternity; appearing
To the Inhabitants of Eden. around them on all sides
But Beulah to its Inhabitants appears within each district
As the beloved infant in his mothers bosom round incircled
With arms of love & pity & sweet compassion. But to
The Sons of Eden the moony habitations of Beulah,
Are from Great Eternity a mild & pleasant Rest.

And it is thus Created. Lo the Eternal Great Humanity
To whom be Glory & Dominion Evermore Amen
Walks among all his awful Family seen in every face
As the breath of the Almighty. such are the Words of man to man
In the great Wars of Eternity, in fury of Poetic Inspiration.
To build the Universe stupendous; Mental forms Creating

But the Emanations trembled exceedingly. nor could they
Live, because the Life of Man was too exceeding unbounded
His joy became terrible to them they trembled & wept
Crying with one voice. Give us a habitation & a place
In which we may be hidden under the shadow of wings
For if we who are but for a time, & who pass away in winter
Behold these wonders of Eternity we shall consume
But you O our Fathers & Brothers, remain in Eternity
But grant us a Temporal Habitation. do you speak
To us; we will obey your words as you obey Jesus
The Eternal who is blessed for ever & ever. Amen

So spake the lovely Emanations; & there appeard a pleasant
Mild Shadow above; beneath; & on all sides round, Into

Into this pleasant Shadow all the weak & weary
Like Women & Children were taken away as on wings
Of dovelike softness. & shadowy habitations prepared for them
But every Man returnd & went still going forward thro'
The Bosom of the Father in Eternity on Eternity
Neither did any lack or fall into Error without
A Shadow to repose in all the Days of happy Eternity

Into this pleasant Shadow Beulah. all Ololon descended
And when the Daughters of Beulah heard the lamentation
All Beulah wept. for they saw the Lord coming in the Clouds
And the Shadows of Beulah terminate in rocky Albion.

And all Nations wept in affliction Family by Family
Germany wept towards France & Italy: England wept & trembled
Towards America: India rose up from his golden bed:
As one awakend in the night: they saw the Lord coming
In the Clouds of Ololon with Power & Great Glory!
And all the Living Creatures of the Four Elements, waild
With bitter wailing: these in the aggregate are named Satan
And Rahab: they know not of Regeneration, but only of Generation
The Fairies, Nymphs, Gnomes & Genii of the Four Elements
Unforgiving, & unalterable: these cannot be Regenerated
But must be Created, for they know only of Generation
These are the Gods of the Kingdoms of the Earth: in contrarious
And cruel opposition: Element against Element, opposed in War
Not Mental, as the Wars of Eternity, but a Corporeal Strife
In Los's Halls continual labouring, in the Furnaces of Golgonooza
Orc howls on the Atlantic: Enitharmon trembles: All Beulah weeps

Thou hearest the Nightingale begin the Song of Spring:
The Lark sitting upon his earthly bed: just as the morn
Appears: listens silent: then springing from the waving Corn-field! loud
He leads the Choir of Day! trill. trill. trill. trill.
Mounting upon the wings of light into the Great Expanse:
Reechoing against the lovely blue & shining heavenly Shell:
His little throat labours with inspiration: every feather
On throat & breast & wings vibrates with the effluence Divine
All Nature listens silent to him, & the awful Sun
Stands still upon the Mountain looking on this little Bird
With eyes of soft humility, & wonder love & awe.
Then loud from their green covert all the Birds begin their Song
The Thrush, the Linnet & the Goldfinch, Robin & the Wren
Awake the Sun from his sweet reverie upon the Mountain:
The Nightingale again assays his song & thro the day
And thro the night warbles luxuriant: every Bird of Song
Attending his loud harmony with admiration & love.
This is a Vision of the lamentation of Beulah over Ololon!

Thou perceivest the Flowers put forth their precious Odours!
And none can tell how from so small a center comes such sweet
Forgetting that within that Center Eternity expands
Its ever during doors, that Og & Anak fiercely guard
First eer the morning breaks joy opens in the flowery bosoms
Joy even to tears, which the Sun-rising dries: first the Wild Thyme
And Meadow-sweet downy & soft waving among the reeds:
Light springing on the air lead the sweet Dance: they wake
The Honeysuckle sleeping on the Oak: the flaunting beauty
Revels along upon the wind: the White-thorn lovely May
Opens her many lovely eyes: listening the Rose still sleeps
None dare to wake her: soon she bursts her crimson curtaind bed
And comes forth in the majesty of beauty: every Flower:
The Pink. the Jessamine, the Wall-flower, the Carnation
The Jonquil, the mild Lilly opes her heavens: every Tree,
And Flower & Herb soon fill the air with an innumerable Dance
Yet all in order sweet & lovely, Men are sick with Love!
Such is a Vision of the lamentation of Beulah over Ololon.

And

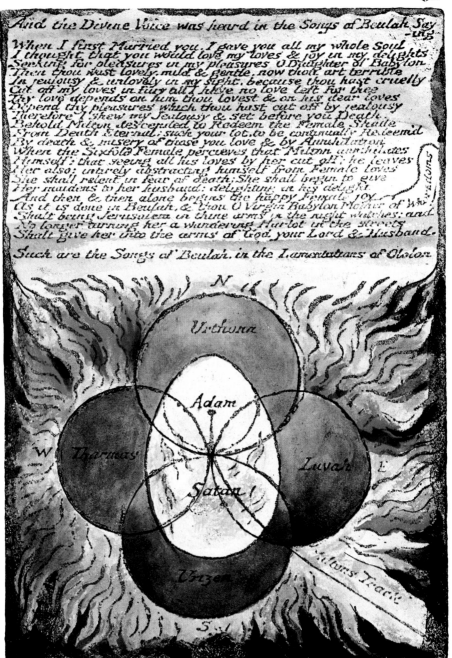

And the Divine Voice was heard in the Songs of Beulah Say
-ing

When I first Married you, I gave you all my whole Soul
I thought that you would love my loves & joy in my delights
Seeking for pleasures in my pleasures O Daughter of Babylon
Then thou wast lovely, mild & gentle, now thou art terrible
In jealousy & unlovely in my sight, because thou hast cruelly
Cut off my loves in fury till I have no love left for thee
Thy love depends on him thou lovest & on his dear loves
Depend thy pleasures which thou hast cut off by jealousy
Therefore I shew my Jealousy & set before you Death.
Behold Milton descended to Redeem the Female Shade
From Death Eternal; such your lot, to be continually Redeemd
By death & misery of those you love & by Annihilation
When the Sixfold Female percieves that Milton annihilates
Himself: that seeing all his loves by her cut off: he leaves
Her also: intirely abstracting himself from Female loves
She shall relent in fear of death; She shall begin to give
Her maidens to her husband: delighting in her delight
And then & then alone begins the happy Female joy
As it is done in Beulah, & thou O Virgin Babylon Mother of Whoredoms
Shalt bring Jerusalem in thine arms in the night watches; and
No longer turning her a wandering Harlot in the streets
Shalt give her into the arms of God your Lord & Husband.

Such are the Songs of Beulah, in the Lamentations of Ololon

And all the Songs of Beulah sounded comfortable notes
To comfort Ololons lamentation, for they said
Are you the Fiery Circle that late drove in fury & fire
The Eight Immortal Starry-Ones down into Ulro dark
Rending the Heavens of Beulah with your thunders & lightnings
And can you thus lament & can you pity & forgive?
Is terror changd to pity, O wonder of Eternity!

And the Four States of Humanity in its Repose,
Were shewed them. First of Beulah a most pleasant Sleep
On Couches soft, with mild music, tended by Flowers of Beulah
Sweet Female forms, winged or floating in the air spontaneous
The Second State is Alla & the third State Al-Ulro;
But the Fourth State is dreadful; it is named Or-Ulro:
The First State is in the Head, the Second is in the Heart:
The Third in the Loins & Seminal Vessels & the Fourth
In the Stomach & Intestines terrible, deadly, unutterable
And he whose Gates are opend in those Regions of his Body
Can from those Gates view all these wondrous Imaginations

But Ololon sought the Or-Ulro & its fiery Gates
And the Couches of the Martyrs: & many Daughters of Beulah
Accompany them down to the Ulro with soft melodious tears
A long journey & dark thro Chaos in the track of Miltons course
To where the Contraries of Beulah War beneath Negations Banner

Then view'd from Miltons Track they see the Ulro: a vast Polypus
Of living fibres down into the Sea of Time & Space growing
A self-devouring monstrous Human Death Twenty-seven fold
Within it sit Five Females & the nameless Shadowy Mother
Spinning it from their bowels with songs of amorous delight
And melting cadences that lure the Sleepers of Beulah down
The River Storge (which is Arnon) into the Dead Sea;
Around this Polypus Los continual builds the Mundane Shell
Four Universes round the Universe of Los remain Chaotic
Four intersecting Globes, & the Egg formd World of Los
In midst; stretching from Zenith to Nadir, in midst of Chaos
One of these Ruind Universes is to the North named Urthona
One to the South, this was the glorious World of Urizen
One to the East, of Luvah: One to the West; of Tharmas,
But when Luvah assumed the World of Urizen in the South
All fell towards the Center sinking downward in dire Ruin

Here in these Chaoses the Sons of Ololon took their abode
In Chasms of the Mundane Shell which open on all sides round
Southward & by the East within the Breach of Miltons descent,
To watch the time, pitying & gentle to awaken Urizen
They stood in a dark land of death of fiery corroding waters
Where lie in evil death the Four Immortals pale and cold
And the Eternal Man even Albion upon the Rock of Ages
Seeing Miltons Shadow, some Daughters of Beulah trembling
Returnd, but Ololon remaind before the Gates of the Dead

And Ololon looked down into the Heavens of Ulro in fear
They said. How are the Wars of Men which in Great Eternity
Appear around, in the External Spheres of Visionary Life
Here renderd Deadly within the Life & Interior Vision
How are the Beasts & Birds & Fishes, & Plants & Minerals
Here fixd into a frozen bulk subject to decay & death
Those Visions of Human Life & Shadows of Wisdom & Knowledge

Are here frozen to unexpansive deadly destroying terrors
And War & Hunting: the Two Fountains of the River of Life
Are become Fountains of bitter Death & of corroding Hell
Till Brotherhood is changd into a Curse & a Flattery
By Differences between Ideas, that Ideas themselves, (which are
The Divine Members) may be slain in offerings for sin
O dreadful Loom of Death! O piteous Female forms compelld
To weave the Woof of Death, On Camberwell Tirzahs Courts
Malahs on Blackheath, Rahab & Noah, dwell on Windsors heights
Where once the Cherubs of Jerusalem spread to Lambeths Vale
Milcahs Pillars shine from Harrow to Hampstead where Hoglah
On Highgates heights magnificent Weaves over trembling Thames
To Shooters Hill and thence to Blackheath the dark Woof! Loud
Loud roll the Weights & Spindles over the whole Earth let down
On all sides round to the Four Quarters of the World, eastward on
Europe to Euphrates & Hindu, to Nile & back in Clouds
Of Death across the Atlantic to America North & South

So spoke Ololon in reminiscence astonishd, but they
Could not behold Golgonooza without passing the Polypus
A wondrous journey not passable by Immortal feet, & none
But the Divine Saviour can pass it without annihilation.
For Golgonooza cannot be seen till having passd the Polypus
It is viewed on all sides round by a Four-fold Vision
Or till you become Mortal & Vegetable in Sexuality
Then you behold its mighty Spires & Domes of ivory & gold

And Ololon examined all the Couches of the Dead.
Even of Los & Enitharmon & all the Sons of Albion
And his Four Zoa's terrified & on the verge of Death
In midst of these was Miltons Couch, & when they saw Eight
Immortal Starry-Ones, guarding the Couch in flaming fires
They thunderous utterd all a universal groan falling down
Prostrate before the Starry Eight asking with tears forgiveness
Confessing their crime with humiliation and sorrow.

O how the Starry Eight rejoic'd to see Ololon descended:
And now that a wide road was open to Eternity,
By Ololons descent thro Beulah to Los & Enitharmon,
For mighty were the multitudes of Ololon, vast the extent
Of their great sway, reaching from Ulro to Eternity
Surrounding the Mundane Shell outside in its Caverns
And through Beulah, and all silent forbore to contend
With Ololon for they saw the Lord in the Clouds of Ololon

There is a Moment in each Day that Satan cannot find
Nor can his Watch Fiends find it, but the Industrious find
This Moment & it multiply, & when it once is found
It renovates every Moment of the Day if rightly placed
In this Moment Ololon descended to Los & Enitharmon
Unseen beyond the Mundane Shell Southward in Miltons track

Just in this Moment when the morning odours rise abroad
And first from the Wild Thyme, stands a Fountain in a rock
Of crystal flowing into two Streams, one flows thro Golgonooza
And thro Beulah to Eden beneath Los's western Wall
The other flows thro the Aerial Void & all the Churches
Meeting again in Golgonooza beyond Satans Seat

The Wild Thyme is Los's Messenger to Eden, a mighty Demon
Terrible deadly & poisonous his presence in Ulro dark
Therefore he appears only a small Root creeping in grass
Covering over the Rock of Odours his bright purple mantle
Beside the Fount above the Larks Nest in Golgonooza
Luvah slept here in death & here is Luvahs empty Tomb
Ololon sat beside this Fountain on the Rock of Odours.

Just at the place to where the Lark mounts, is a Crystal Gate
It is the enterance of the First Heaven named Luther: for
The Lark is Los's Messenger thro the Twenty-seven Churches
That the Seven Eyes of God who walk even to Satans Seat
Thro all the Twenty-seven Heavens may not slumber nor sleep
But the Larks Nest is at the Gate of Los, at the eastern
Gate of wide Golgonooza & the Lark is Los's Messenger

When on the highest lift of his light pinions he arrives
At that bright Gate. another Lark meets him & back to back
They touch their pinions tip tip: and each descend
To their respective Earths & there all night consult with Angels
Of Providence & with the Eyes of God all night in slumbers
Inspired: & at the dawn of day send out another Lark
Into another Heaven to carry news upon his wings
Thus are the Messengers dispatchd till they reach the Earth again
In the East Gate of Golgonooza, & the Twenty-eighth bright
Lark. met the Female Ololon descending into my Garden
Thus it appears to Mortal eyes & those of the Ulro Heavens
But not thus to Immortals, the Lark is a mighty Angel.

For Ololon step'd into the Polypus within the Mundane Shell
They could not step into Vegetable Worlds without becoming
The enemies of Humanity except in a Female Form
And as One Female. Ololon and all its mighty Hosts
Appear'd: a Virgin of twelve years nor time nor space was
To the perception of the Virgin Ololon but as the
Flash of lightning but more quick the Virgin in my Garden
Before my Cottage stood for the Satanic Space is delusion.

For when Los joind with me he took me in his fiery whirlwind
My Vegetated portion was hurried from Lambeths shades
He set me down in Felphams Vale & prepard a beautiful
Cottage for me that in three years I might write all these
    Visions
To display Natures cruel holiness: the deceits of Natural
    Religion
Walking in my Cottage Garden, sudden I beheld
The Virgin Ololon & addressd her as a Daughter of Beulah
Virgin of Providence fear not to enter into my Cottage
What is thy message to thy friend: what am I now to do
Is it again to plunge into deeper affliction? behold me
Ready to obey, but pity thou my Shadow of Delight
Enter my Cottage. comfort her, for she is sick with fatigue

Blakes Cottage
at Felpham.

The Virgin answerd. Knowest thou of Milton who descended
Driven from Eternity; him I seek! terrified at my Act
In Great Eternity which thou knowest: I come him to seek

So Ololon utterd in words distinct the anxious thought
Mild was the voice, but more distinct than any earthly
That Miltons Shadow heard &, condensing all his Fibres
Into a strength impregnable of majesty & beauty infinite
I saw he was the Covering Cherub & within him Satan
And Rahab, in an outside which is fallacious; within,
Beyond the outline of Identity, in the Selfhood deadly
And he appeard the Wicker Man of Scandinavia in whom
Jerusalems children consume in flames among the Stars

Descending down into my Garden, a Human Wonder of God
Reaching from heaven to earth, a Cloud & Human Form
I beheld Milton with astonishment & in him beheld
The Monstrous Churches of Beulah, the Gods of Ulro dark
Twelve monstrous dishumanized terrors Synagogues of Satan.
A Double Twelve & Thrice Nine: such their divisions.

And these their Names & their Places within the Mundane Shell
In Tyre & Sidon I saw Baal & Ashtaroth. In Moab Chemosh
In Ammon, Molech: loud his Furnaces rage among the Wheels
Of Og, & pealing loud the cries of the Victims of Fire:
And pale his Priestesses unfolded in Veils of Pestilence, border'd
With War: Woven in Looms of Tyre & Sidon by beautiful Ashtaroth
In Palestine Dagon, Sea Monster: worshipd o'er the Sea.
Thammuz, in Lebanon & Rimmon in Damascus curtaind
Osiris: Isis: Orus: in Egypt: dark their Tabernacles on Nile
Floating with solemn songs, & on the Lakes of Egypt nightly
With pomp, even till morning break & Osiris appear in the sky
But Belial of Sodom & Gomorrha, obscure Demon of Bribes
And secret Assassinations, not worshipd nor adord: but
With the finger on the lips & the back turnd to the light
And Saturn Jove & Rhea of the Isles of the Sea remote
These Twelve Gods, are the Twelve Spectre Sons of the Druid Albion

And these the Names of the Twenty-seven Heavens & their Churches
Adam, Seth, Enos, Cainan, Mahalaleel, Jared, Enoch,
Methuselah, Lamech: these are Giants mighty Hermaphroditic
Noah, Shem, Arphaxad, Cainan the second, Salah, Heber
Peleg, Reu, Serug, Nahor, Terah, these are the Female Males
A Male within a Female hid as in an Ark & Curtains,
Abraham, Moses, Solomon, Paul, Constantine, Charlemaine
Luther, these seven are the Male Females, the Dragon Forms
Religion hid in War, a Dragon red & hidden Harlot

All these are seen in Miltons Shadow who is the Covering Cherub
The Spectre of Albion in which the Spectre of Luvah inhabits
In the Newtonian Voids between the Substances of Creation

For the Chaotic Voids outside of the Stars are measured by
The Stars, which are the boundaries of Kingdoms, Provinces
And Empires of Chaos invisible to the Vegetable Man
The Kingdom of Og, is in Orion: Sihon is in Ophiucus
Og has Twenty-seven Districts; Sihons Districts Twenty-one
From Star to Star, Mountains & Valleys, terrible dimension
Stretchd out, compose the Mundane Shell, a mighty Incrustation
Of Forty-eight deformed Human Wonders of the Almighty
With Caverns whose remotest bottoms meet again beyond
The Mundane Shell in Golgonooza, but the Fires of Los, rage
In the remotest bottoms of the Caves, that none can pass
Into Eternity that way, but all descend to Los
To Bowlahoola & Allamanda & to Entuthon Benython
The Heavens are the Cherub, the Twelve Gods are Satan

And the Forty-eight Starry Regions are Cities of the Levites
The Heads of the Great Polypus. Four-fold twelve enormity
In mighty & mysterious comingling enemy with enemy
Woven by Urizen into Sexes from his mantle of years
And Milton collecting all his fibres into impregnable strength
Descended down a Paved work of all kinds of precious stones
Out from the eastern sky; descending down into my Cottage
Garden: clothed in black, severe & silent he descended.

The Spectre of Satan stood upon the roaring sea & beheld
Milton within his sleeping Humanity; trembling & shuddring
He stood upon the waves a Twenty-seven-fold mighty Demon
Gorgeous & beautiful: loud roll his thunders against Milton
Loud Satan thunderd, loud, & dark upon mild Felpham Shore
Not daring to touch one fibre he howld round upon the Sea.

I also stood in Satans bosom & beheld its desolations:
A ruind Man: a ruind building of God not made with hands;
Its plains of burning sand, its mountains of marble terrible:
Its pits & declivities flowing with molten ore & fountains
Of pitch & nitre; its ruind palaces & cities & mighty works;
Its furnaces of affliction in which his Angels & Emanations
Labour with blackend visages among its stupendous ruins
Arches & pyramids & porches colonades & domes:
In which dwells Mystery Babylon, here is her secret place
From hence she comes forth on the Churches in delight
Here is her Cup filld with its poisons, in these horrid vales
And here her scarlet Veil woven in pestilence & war:
Here is Jerusalem bound in chains, in the Dens of Babylon

In the Eastern porch of Satans Universe Milton stood & said

Satan! my Spectre! I know my power thee to annihilate
And be a greater in thy place, & be thy Tabernacle
A covering for thee to do thy will, till one greater comes
And smites me as I smote thee & becomes my covering
Such are the Laws of thy false Heavns: but Laws of Eternity
Are not such: know thou: I come to Self Annihilation
Such are the Laws of Eternity that each shall mutually
Annihilate himself for others good, as I for thee
Thy purpose & the purpose of thy Priests & of thy Churches
Is to impress on men the fear of death; to teach
Trembling & fear, terror, constriction; abject selfishness
Mine is to teach Men to despise death & to go on
In fearless majesty annihilating Self, laughing to scorn
Thy Laws & terrors, shaking down thy Synagogues as webs
I come to discover before Heavn & Hell the Self righteousness
In all its Hypocritic turpitude, opening to every eye
These wonders of Satans holiness shewing to the Earth
The Idol Virtues of the Natural Heart, & Satans Seat
Explore in all its Selfish Natural Virtue & put off
In Self annihilation all that is not of God alone:
To put off Self & all I have ever & ever Amen

Satan heard! Coming in a cloud, with trumpets & flaming fire
Saying I am God the judge of all, the living & the dead
Fall therefore down & worship me, submit thy supreme
Dictate, to my eternal Will & to my dictate bow
I hold the Balances of Right & Just & mine the Sword
Seven Angels bear my Name & in those Seven I appear
But I alone am God & I alone in Heavn & Earth
Of all that live dare utter this, others tremble & bow

Till All Things became One Great Satan, in Holiness
Opposd to Mercy, and the Divine Delusion Jesus be no more

Suddenly around Milton on my Path, the Starry Seven
Burnd terrible: my Path became a solid fire, as bright
As the clear Sun & Milton silent came down on my Path.
And there went forth from the Starry limbs of the Seven: Forms
Human; with Trumpets innumerable, sounding articulate
As the Seven spake; and they stood in a mighty Column of Fire
Surrounding Felphams Vale, reaching to the Mundane Shell, Saying

Awake Albion awake! reclaim thy Reasoning Spectre, Subdue
Him to the Divine Mercy, Cast him down into the Lake
Of Los, that ever burneth with fire, ever & ever Amen!
Let the Four Zoas awake from Slumbers of Six Thousand Years

Then loud the Furnaces of Los were heard, & seen as Seven Heavens
Stretching from south to north over the mountains of Albion

Satan heard, trembling round his Body, he incircled it
He trembled with exceeding great trembling & astonishment
Howling in his Spectre round his Body hungring to devour
But fearing for the pain for if he touches a Vital,
His torment is unendurable: therefore he cannot devour:
But howls round it as a lion round his prey continually
Loud Satan thundered, loud & dark upon mild Felphams Shore
Coming in a Cloud with Trumpets & with Fiery Flame
An awful Form eastward from midst of a bright Paved-work
Of precious stones by Cherubim surrounded: so permitted
(Lest he should fall apart in his Eternal Death) to imitate
The Eternal Great Humanity Divine surrounded by
His Cherubim & Seraphim in ever happy Eternity
Beneath sat Chaos: Sin on his right hand Death on his left
And Ancient Night spread over all the heavn his Mantle of Laws
He trembled with exceeding great trembling & astonishment

Then Albion rose up in the Night of Beulah on his Couch
Of dread repose seen by the visionary eye: his face is toward
The east, toward Jerusalems Gates: groaning he sat above
His rocks, London & Bath & Legions & Edinburgh
Are the four pillars of his Throne; his left foot near London
Covers the shades of Tyburn; his instep from Windsor
To Primrose Hill stretching to Highgate & Holloway
London is between his knees; its basements fourfold
His right foot stretches to the sea on Dover cliffs, his heel
On Canterburys ruins; his right hand covers lofty Wales
His left Scotland; his bosom girt with gold involves
York, Edinburgh, Durham & Carlisle & on the front
Bath, Oxford, Cambridge Norwich; his right elbow
Leans on the Rocks of Erins Land, Ireland ancient nation
His head bends over London: he sees his embodied Spectre
Trembling before him with exceeding great trembling & fear
He views Jerusalem & Babylon, his tears flow down
He movd his right foot to Cornwall, his left to the Rocks of Bognor
He strove to rise to walk into the Deep, but strength failing
Forbad & down with dreadful groans he sunk upon his Couch
In moony Beulah, Los his strong Guard walks round beneath the Moon

Urizen faints in terror striving among the Brooks of Arnon
With Miltons Spirit: as the Plowman or Artificer or Shepherd
While in the labours of his Calling sends his Thought abroad
To labour in the ocean or in the starry heaven. So Milton
Labourd in Chasms of the Mundane Shell, tho here before
My Cottage midst the Starry Seven, where the Virgin Ololon
Stood trembling in the Porch: loud Satan thundered on the stormy Sea
Circling Albions Cliffs in which the Four-fold World resides
Tho seen in fallacy outside: a fallacy of Satans Churches

Before Ololon Milton stood & percievd the Eternal Form
Of that mild Vision; wondrous were their acts by me unknown
Except remotely; and I heard Ololon say to Milton.

I see thee strive upon the Brooks of Arnon. there a dread
And awful Man I see, oercoverd with the mantle of years.
I behold Los & Urizen. I behold Orc & Tharmas;
The Four Zoa's of Albion & thy Spirit with them striving
In Self annihilation giving thy life to thy enemies
Are those who contemn Religion & seek to annihilate it
Become in their Feminine portions, the causes & promoters
Of these Religions, how is this thing? this Newtonian Phantasm
This Voltaire & Rousseau: this Hume & Gibbon & Bolingbroke
This Natural Religion! this impossible absurdity
Is Ololon the cause of this? O where shall I hide my face
These tears fall for the little-ones: the Children of Jerusalem.
Lest they be annihilated in thy annihilation.

No sooner she had spoke but Rahab Babylon appeard
Eastward upon the Paved work across Europe & Asia
Glorious as the midday Sun in Satans bosom glowing:
A Female hidden in a Male, Religion hidden in War
Namd Moral Virtue; cruel two-fold Monster shining bright
A Dragon red & hidden Harlot which John in Patmos saw

And all beneath the Nations innumerable of Ulro
Appeard, the Seven Kingdoms of Canaan & Five Baalim
Of Philistea, into Twelve divided, calld after the Names
Of Israel: as they are in Eden. Mountain River & Plain
City & sandy Desert intermingled beyond mortal ken

But turning toward Ololon in terrible majesty Milton
Replied. Obey thou the Words of the Inspired Man.
All that can be annihilated must be annihilated
That the Children of Jerusalem may be saved from slavery
There is a Negation, & there is a Contrary
The Negation must be destroyd to redeem the Contraries
The Negation is the Spectre; the Reasoning Power in Man
This is a false Body: an Incrustation over my Immortal
Spirit; a Selfhood, which must be put off & annihilated alway
To cleanse the Face of my Spirit by Self-examination.

To bathe in the Waters of Life; to wash off the Not Human
I come in Self-annihilation & the grandeur of Inspiration
To cast off Rational Demonstration by Faith in the Saviour
To cast off the rotten rags of Memory by Inspiration
To cast off Bacon, Locke & Newton from Albions covering
To take off his filthy garments, & clothe him with Imagination
To cast aside from Poetry, all that is not Inspiration
That it no longer shall dare to mock with the aspersion of Madness
Cast on the Inspired, by the tame high finisher of paltry Blots,
Indefinite, or paltry Rhymes; or paltry Harmonies,
Who creeps into State Government like a caterpiller to destroy
To cast off the idiot Questioner who is always questioning,
But never capable of answering; who sits with a sly grin
Silent plotting when to question, like a thief in a cave;
Who publishes doubt & calls it knowledge; whose Science is Despair
Whose pretence to knowledge is Envy; whose whole Science is
To destroy the wisdom of ages to gratify ravenous Envy,
That rages round him like a Wolf day & night without rest
He smiles with condescension; he talks of Benevolence & Virtue
And those who act with Benevolence & Virtue, they murder time on time
These are the destroyers of Jerusalem, these are the murderers
Of Jesus, who deny the Faith & mock at Eternal Life:
Who pretend to Poetry that they may destroy Imagination;
By imitation of Natures Images drawn from Remembrance
These are the Sexual Garments, the Abomination of Desolation
Hiding the Human Lineaments as with an Ark & Curtains
Which Jesus rent: & now shall wholly purge away with Fire
Till Generation is swallowd up in Regeneration.

Then trembled the Virgin Ololon & replyd in clouds of despair
Is this our Feminine Portion the Six-fold Miltonic Female
Terribly this Portion trembles before thee O awful Man
Altho our Human Power can sustain the severe contentions
Of Friendship, our Sexual cannot: but flies into the Ulro.
Hence arose all our terrors in Eternity! & now remembrance
Returns upon us! are we Contraries O Milton, Thou & I
O Immortal! how were we led to War the Wars of Death
Is this the Void Outside of Existence, which if enterd into

Becomes a Womb, & is this the Death Couch of Albion
Thou goest to Eternal Death & all must go with thee!

So saying, the Virgin divided Six-fold & with a shriek
Dolorous that ran thro all Creation a Double-Six-fold Wonder!
Away from Ololon she divided & fled into the depths
Of Miltons Shadow as a Dove upon the stormy Sea.

Then as a Moony Ark Ololon descended to Felphams Vale
In clouds of blood, in streams of gore, with dreadful thunderings
Into the Fires of Intellect that rejoic'd in Felphams Vale
Around the Starry Eight: with one accord the Starry Eight became
One Man Jesus the Saviour. wonderful! round his limbs
The Clouds of Ololon folded as a Garment dipped in blood
Written within & without in woven letters: & the Writing
Is the Divine Revelation in the Litteral expression:
A Garment of War, I heard it namd the Woof of Six Thousand Years

And I beheld the Twenty-four Cities of Albion
Arise upon their Thrones to Judge the Nations of the Earth
And the Immortal Four in whom the Twenty-four appear Four-fold
Arose around Albions body: Jesus wept & walked forth
From Felphams Vale clothed in Clouds of blood, to enter into
Albions Bosom, the bosom of death, & the Four surrounded him
In the Column of Fire in Felphams Vale; then to their mouths the Four
Applied their Four Trumpets & them sounded to the Four winds

Terror struck in the Vale I stood at that immortal sound
My bones trembled, I fell outstretchd upon the path
A moment, & my Soul returned into its mortal state
To Resurrection & Judgment in the Vegetable Body
And my sweet Shadow of Delight stood trembling by my side

Immediately the Lark mounted with a loud trill from Felphams Vale
And the Wild Thyme from Wimbletons green & impurpled Hills
And Los & Enitharmon rose over the Hills of Surrey
Their Clouds roll over London with a south wind, soft Oothoon
Pants in the Vales of Lambeth weeping oer her Human Harvest
Los listens to the Cry of the Poor Man: his Cloud
Over London in volume terrific, low bended in anger.

Rintrah & Palamabron view the Human Harvest beneath
Their Wine-presses & Barns stand open; the Ovens are prepar'd
The Waggons ready: terrific Lions & Tygers sport & play
All Animals upon the Earth, are prepard in all their strength

To go forth to the Great Harvest & Vintage
of the Nations

Finis

PART TWO

TEXT

TEXTUAL NOTE

IN the following transcription of *Milton*, plates 1 through 45 of Copy B from The Huntington Library and plates a through f of Copy D from the Lessing J. Rosenwald Collection of The Library of Congress, we have normalized Blake's punctuation for reading convenience. We have normalized Blake's spelling only when, in our opinion, his spelling interferes with current reading habits. We have attempted accurate reproduction of Blake's capitalization in Copy B and in the six plates of Copy D, altering capitalization only when change in, or addition of, a mark of punctuation necessitated such alteration. We stress that this is not intended to be a definitive text; it is a reading text. Each reader of *Milton* should experiment with his or her own perceptions of Blake's punctuation, spelling, and capitalization, especially since the nature of the punctuation often shapes the reader's perception of the meaning of Blake's words.

As Blake tells us in *Milton*, the inspiration for the poem came as the result of a vision, during which Milton and Los appeared to him in Lambeth. Since, as Blake also records in *Milton*, Los took him from Lambeth to Felpham, and since Blake lived in Felpham from September 1800 to September 1803, in a beautiful cottage under the patronage of William Hayley, this initial inspiration came prior to 1800. Thus, in all probability, Blake was composing *Milton* from 1800 to 1803, and the 1804 date on the title-page may acknowledge his completion of composition. However, he did not print *Milton* before 1808 or 1809 as Copies A, B, and C are on paper watermarked 1808. The earliest copies, A and B, have 45 plates, including the "Preface"; Copy C, on the other hand, contains 5 additional text plates (a, b, d, e, f); while Copy D, on paper watermarked 1815, contains the plates added to Copy C and one more, plate c. Moreover, both Copy C and Copy D lack the "Preface," and in Copies C and D the plates numbered 24, 25, 26 in Copies A and B are rearranged, as 26, 24, and 25 in Copy C and as 29, 27, and 28 in Copy D. Also in Copies C and D, the full-page design, which is plate 21 in Copies A and B, is moved to become plate 43 in Copy C and plate 47 in Copy D. Therefore, given the four copies of *Milton*, their arrangements and approximate dates, Blake apparently reworked *Milton* through 1815 or 1816. Because we wish to give a sense of all versions of *Milton*, and yet maintain the integrity of Copy B, we have separated the plates of Copies B and D, placing the reproductions from D in an appendix following the Commentary, but we have inserted the transcribed text of each of the plates from Copy D, a through f, within the transcription of Copy B. Since Copy D has been rebound too tightly to permit color photography, plates a through f, unfortunately, appear in monochrome. Our commentary on *Milton* is based on a "complete" copy of 51 plates; however, no one of the four existing copies has all 51.

That a typographic text is an inadequate representation of Blake's vision is obvious. Blake printed his work by a method of relief etching taught him by the spirit of his brother, Robert, some time after Robert's death in 1787. In fact, Blake acknowledges that he writes from Robert's "Dictate" in plate 33 of *Milton*. By this method, Blake's words and designs were raised in relief from the surface of a copperplate. Blake describes the method metaphorically in *The Marriage of Heaven and Hell* where "by corrosives"—the acid of the etching process—the "apparent surfaces" of rational vision are melted away to display "the infinite which was hid."

Scholars still debate the minute particulars of Blake's method; it seems, however, that Blake either wrote backwards on the copperplate in an acid-resistant varnish or that he transferred his letters from a specially prepared piece of paper to a heated copperplate in a manner comparable to transferring an embroidery design to cloth. Blake perhaps drew his designs directly on the copperplate, in reverse. The plate was then immersed in an acid bath for six to eight hours where the unprotected background was dissolved, leaving the acid-resistant lettering and design in relief. When Blake removed the plate from the acid bath, he laboriously perfected the words and designs; thus the plate was ready for inking and printing. Apparently, Blake inked another unbitten copperplate and pressed it against the etched plate transferring the ink to the relief surfaces. He then took a sheet of paper, placed it against the relief-etched plate and, using an engraver's rolling press, printed the etching upon the paper. Then, he often touched up and colored the prints, so that each one was an individual work of art. As Blake's biographer, Alexander Gilchrist, aptly noted, "never before surely was a man so literally the author of his own book." Blake's unique method of intermingling poetry with design results in a unique reading predicament, for each copy of a single work is different; each is a new version of the poem, whole and complete. Thus, Blake's reader must see *Milton* anew in Copy A or Copy B or Copy C or Copy D. Blake has prepared carefully the reading experience so as to provoke a cleansing of the "doors of perception," that his reader might see "the infinite in all things."

[PLATE 1]

MILTON

a Poem in 2 Books

The Author & Printer W Blake 1804

To Justify the Ways of God to Men

[PLATE 2]

PREFACE

THE Stolen and Perverted Writings of Homer & Ovid, of Plato & Cicero, which all Men ought to contemn, are set up by artifice against the Sublime of the Bible; but, when the New Age is at leisure to Pronounce, all will be set right, & those Grand Works of the more ancient & consciously & professedly Inspired Men will hold their proper rank, & the Daughters of Memory shall become the Daughters of Inspiration. Shakspeare & Milton were both curb'd by the general malady & infection from the silly Greek & Latin slaves of the Sword. Rouze up, O Young Men of the New Age! Set your foreheads against the ignorant Hirelings! For we have Hirelings in the Camp, the Court & the University, who would, if they could, forever depress Mental & prolong Corporeal War. Painters, on you I call! Sculptors! Architects! Suffer not the fashionable Fools to depress your powers by the prices they pretend to give for contemptible works or the expensive advertizing boasts that they make of such works; believe Christ & his Apostles that there is a Class of Men whose whole delight is in Destroying. We do not want either Greek or Roman Models if we are but just & true to our own Imaginations, those Worlds of Eternity in which we shall live forever in Jesus our Lord.

And did those feet in ancient time
Walk upon England's mountains green?
And was the holy Lamb of God,
On England's pleasant pastures seen?

And did the Countenance Divine
Shine forth upon our clouded hills?
And was Jerusalem builded here
Among these dark Satanic Mills?

Bring me my Bow of burning gold;
Bring me my Arrows of desire;
Bring me my Spear; O clouds unfold!
Bring me my Chariot of fire!

I will not cease from Mental Fight,
Nor shall my Sword sleep in my hand,
Till we have built Jerusalem
In England's green & pleasant Land.

———————————

Would to God that all the Lord's people were Prophets.
Numbers, XI. ch., 29 v.

[PLATE 3]

MILTON

Book the First

Daughters of Beulah! Muses who inspire the Poet's Song,
Record the journey of immortal Milton thro' your Realms
Of terror & mild moony lustre, in soft sexual delusions
Of varied beauty, to delight the wanderer and repose
His burning thirst & freezing hunger! Come into my hand
By your mild power descending down the Nerves of my right arm
From out the Portals of my Brain, where by your ministry
The Eternal Great Humanity Divine planted his Paradise,
And in it caus'd the Spectres of the Dead to take sweet forms
In likeness of himself. Tell also of the False Tongue, vegetated
Beneath your land of shadows, of its sacrifices, and
Its offerings, even till Jesus, the image of the Invisible God,
Became its prey: a curse, an offering, and an atonement
For Death Eternal in the heavens of Albion & before the Gates
Of Jerusalem, his Emanation, in the heavens beneath Beulah.

Say first! what mov'd Milton—who walk'd about in Eternity
One hundred years, pondering the intricate mazes of Providence,
Unhappy tho' in heav'n, he obey'd, he murmur'd not, he was silent
Viewing his Sixfold Emanation scatter'd thro' the deep
In torment—to go into the deep her to redeem & himself perish?
What cause at length mov'd Milton to this unexampled deed?
A Bard's prophetic Song! For, sitting at eternal tables,
Terrific among the Sons of Albion in chorus solemn & loud,
A Bard broke forth! All sat attentive to the awful man.

Mark well my words; they are of your eternal salvation!

Three Classes are Created by the Hammer of Los & Woven

[PLATE a, PLATE 3 in Copy D]

By Enitharmon's Looms when Albion was slain upon his Mountains
And in his Tent, thro' envy of Living Form, even of the Divine Vision
And of the sports of Wisdom in the Human Imagination,
Which is the Divine Body of the Lord Jesus, Blessed for ever.
Mark well my words; they are of your eternal salvation!

Urizen lay in darkness & solitude, in chains of the mind lock'd up.
Los seiz'd his Hammer & Tongs; he labour'd at his resolute Anvil
Among indefinite Druid rocks & snows of doubt & reasoning.

Refusing all Definite Form, the Abstract Horror roof'd, stony hard,
And a first Age passed over & a State of dismal woe.

Down sunk with fright a red round Globe hot burning, deep,
Deep down into the Abyss, panting, conglobing, trembling,
And a second Age passed over & a State of dismal woe.

Rolling round into two little Orbs & closed in two little Caves,
The Eyes beheld the Abyss, lest bones of solidness freeze over all,
And a third Age passed over & a State of dismal woe.

From beneath his Orbs of Vision, Two Ears in close volutions
Shot spiring out in the deep darkness & petrified as they grew,
And a fourth Age passed over & a State of dismal woe.

Hanging upon the wind, Two Nostrils bent down into the Deep,
And a fifth Age passed over & a State of dismal woe.

In ghastly torment sick, a Tongue of hunger & thirst flamed out,
And a sixth Age passed over & a State of dismal woe.

Enraged & stifled without & within, in terror & woe, he threw his
Right Arm to the north, his left Arm to the south, & his Feet

Stamp'd the nether Abyss in trembling & howling & dismay,
And a seventh Age passed over & a State of dismal woe.

Terrified Los stood in the Abyss, & his immortal limbs
Grew deadly pale; he became what he beheld: for a red
Round Globe sunk down from his Bosom into the Deep; in pangs
He hover'd over it trembling & weeping; suspended, it shook
The nether Abyss in tremblings; he wept over it, he cherish'd it
In deadly sickening pain, till separated into a Female pale
As the cloud that brings the snow; all the while from his Back
A blue fluid exuded in Sinews, hardening in the Abyss,
Till it separated into a Male Form howling in Jealousy.

Within labouring, beholding Without, from Particulars to Generals
Subduing his Spectre, they Builded the Looms of Generation;
They Builded Great Golgonooza Times on Times, Ages on Ages.
First Orc was Born, then the Shadowy Female, then all Los's Family.
At last Enitharmon brought forth Satan Refusing Form in vain:
The Miller of Eternity made subservient to the Great Harvest,
That he may go to his own Place, Prince of the Starry Wheels,

[PLATE b, PLATE 4 in Copy D]
Beneath the Plow of Rintrah & the Harrow of the Almighty
In the hands of Palamabron, Where the Starry Mills of Satan
Are built beneath the Earth & Waters of the Mundane Shell.
Here the Three Classes of Men take their Sexual texture, Woven.
The Sexual is Threefold; the Human is Fourfold.

"If you account it Wisdom when you are angry to be silent, and
Not to shew it, I do not account that Wisdom, but Folly.
Every Man's Wisdom is peculiar to his own Individuality.
O Satan, my youngest born, art thou not Prince of the Starry Hosts
And of the Wheels of Heaven, to turn the Mills day & night?
Art thou not Newton's Pantocrator, weaving the Woof of Locke?

To Mortals thy Mills seem every thing, & the Harrow of Shaddai
A scheme of Human conduct invisible & incomprehensible.
Get to thy Labours at the Mills & leave me to my wrath.''

Satan was going to reply, but Los roll'd his loud thunders:
"Anger me not! thou canst not drive the Harrow in pity's paths.
Thy Work is Eternal Death with Mills & Ovens & Cauldrons.
Trouble me no more; thou canst not have Eternal Life.''

So Los spoke! Satan trembling obey'd, weeping along the way.
Mark well my words; they are of your eternal Salvation!

Between South Molton Street & Stratford Place, Calvary's foot,
Where the Victims were preparing for Sacrifice their Cherubim
Around their loins pour'd forth their arrows, & their bosoms beam
With all colours of precious stones, & their inmost palaces
Resounded with preparation of animals wild & tame
(Mark well my words! Corporeal Friends are Spiritual Enemies),
Mocking Druidical Mathematical Proportion of Length, Bredth,
    Highth,
Displaying Naked Beauty, with Flute & Harp & Song!

[PLATE c, PLATE 5 in Copy D]
Palamabron with the fiery Harrow in morning returning
From breathing fields, Satan fainted beneath the artillery,
Christ took on Sin in the Virgin's Womb, & put it off on the Cross.
All pitied the piteous & was wrath with the wrathful, & Los heard it.

And this is the manner of the Daughters of Albion in their beauty.
Every one is threefold in Head & Heart & Reins, & every one
Has three Gates into the Three Heavens of Beulah, which shine
Translucent in their Foreheads & their Bosoms & their Loins
Surrounded with fires unapproachable; but whom they please
They take up into their Heavens in intoxicating delight,

For the Elect cannot be Redeem'd, but Created continually
By Offering & Atonement in the cruelties of Moral Law.
Hence the three Classes of Men take their fix'd destinations.
They are the two Contraries & the Reasoning Negative.

While the Females prepare the Victims, the Males at Furnaces
And Anvils dance the dance of tears & pain; loud lightnings
Lash on their limbs as they turn the whirlwinds loose upon
The Furnaces, lamenting around the Anvils, & this their Song:

"Ah weak & wide astray! Ah shut in narrow doleful form,
Creeping in reptile flesh upon the bosom of the ground:
The Eye of Man a little narrow orb, clos'd up & dark,
Scarcely beholding the great light, conversing with the Void;
The Ear a little shell, in small volutions shutting out
All melodies & comprehending only Discord and Harmony;
The tongue a little moisture fills, a little food it cloys,
A little sound it utters & its cries are faintly heard,
Then brings forth Moral Virtue the cruel Virgin Babylon.

Can such an Eye Judge of the stars? & looking thro' its tubes
Measure the sunny rays that point their spears on Udanadan?
Can such an Ear, fill'd with the vapours of the yawning pit,
Judge of the pure melodious harp struck by a hand divine?
Can such closed Nostrils feel a joy? or tell of autumn fruits
When grapes & figs burst their covering to the joyful air?
Can such a Tongue boast of the living waters? or take in
Ought but the Vegetable Ratio & loathe the faint delight?
Can such gross Lips percieve? alas, folded within themselves
They touch not ought, but pallid turn & tremble at every wind."

Thus they sing Creating the Three Classes among Druid Rocks.
Charles calls on Milton for Atonement. Cromwell is ready.
James calls for fires in Golgonooza, for heaps of smoking ruins

In the night of prosperity and wantonness which he himself Created
Among the Daughters of Albion, among the rocks of the Druids
When Satan fainted beneath the arrows of Elynittria
And Mathematic Proportion was subdued by Living Proportion.

[PLATE 4]

From Golgonooza, the spiritual Fourfold London eternal,
In immense labours & sorrows, ever building, ever falling,
Thro' Albion's four Forests which overspread all the Earth:
From London Stone to Blackheath east, to Hounslow west,
To Finchely north, to Norwood south; and the weights
Of Enitharmon's Loom play lulling cadences on the winds of Albion
From Caithness in the north to Lizard-point & Dover in the south.

Loud sounds the Hammer of Los, & loud his Bellows is heard
Before London to Hampstead's breadths & Highgate's heights, to
Stratford & old Bow, & across to the Gardens of Kensington
On Tyburn's Brook; loud groans Thames beneath the iron Forge
Of Rintrah & Palamabron, of Theotormon & Bromion, to forge
        the instruments
Of Harvest: the Plow & Harrow to pass over the Nations.

The Surrey hills glow like the clinkers of the furnace;
        Lambeth's Vale—
Where Jerusalem's foundations began, where they were laid in ruins,
Where they were laid in ruins from every Nation & Oak Groves
        rooted—
Dark gleams before the Furnace-mouth a heap of burning ashes.
When shall Jerusalem return & overspread all the Nations?
Return, return to Lambeth's Vale, O building of human souls!
Thence stony Druid Temples overspread the island white,
And thence from Jerusalem's ruins, from her walls of salvation
And praise, thro' the whole Earth were rear'd—from Ireland
To Mexico & Peru west, & east to China & Japan—till Babel,

The Spectre of Albion, frown'd over the Nations in glory & war.
All things begin & end in Albion's ancient Druid rocky shore;
But now the Starry Heavens are fled from the mighty limbs of Albion.

Loud sounds the Hammer of Los, loud turn the Wheels of
    Enitharmon:
Her Looms vibrate with soft affections, weaving the Web of Life
Out from the ashes of the dead; Los lifts his iron Ladles
With molten ore; he heaves the iron cliffs in his rattling chains
From Hyde Park to the Alms-houses of Mile-end & old Bow.
Here the Three Classes of Mortal Men take their fix'd destinations,
And hence they overspread the Nations of the whole Earth, & hence
The Web of Life is woven, & the tender sinews of life created
And the Three Classes of Men regulated by Los's Hammer and woven

[PLATE 5]
By Enitharmon's Looms & Spun beneath the Spindle of Tirzah:
The first, the Elect from before the foundation of the World;
The second, the Redeem'd; the Third, the Reprobate & form'd
To destruction from the mother's womb.
                            Follow with me my plow.

Of the first class was Satan: with incomparable mildness,
His primitive tyrannical attempts on Los, with most endearing love
He soft intreated Los to give to him Palamabron's station,
For Palamabron return'd with labour wearied every evening.
Palamabron oft refus'd and, as often, Satan offer'd
His service, till by repeated offers and repeated intreaties
Los gave to him the Harrow of the Almighty; alas, blamable,
Palamabron fear'd to be angry lest Satan should accuse him of
Ingratitude, & Los believe the accusation thro' Satan's extreme
Mildness. Satan labour'd all day—it was a thousand years—
In the evening returning terrified, overlabour'd & astonish'd,
Embrac'd soft with a brother's tears Palamabron, who also wept.

Mark well my words; they are of your eternal salvation!

Next morning, Palamabron rose: the horses of the Harrow
Were madden'd with tormenting fury, & the servants of the Harrow,
The Gnomes, accus'd Satan, with indignation, fury, and fire.
Then Palamabron, reddening like the Moon in an eclipse,
Spoke, saying, "You know Satan's mildness and his self-imposition,
Seeming a brother, being a tyrant, even thinking himself a brother
While he is murdering the just; prophetic I behold
His future course thro' darkness and despair to eternal death.
But we must not be tyrants also! He hath assum'd my place
For one whole day, under pretence of pity and love to me!
My horses hath he madden'd and my fellow servants injur'd.
How should he, he, know the duties of another? O foolish forbearance!
Would I had told Los all my heart! But patience, O my friends,
All may be well: silent remain, while I call Los and Satan."

Loud as the wind of Beulah that unroots the rocks & hills
Palamabron call'd, and Los & Satan came before him,
And Palamabron shew'd the horses & the servants. Satan wept,
And mildly cursing Palamabron, him accus'd of crimes
Himself had wrought. Los trembled; Satan's blandishments almost
Persuaded the Prophet of Eternity that Palamabron
Was Satan's enemy & that the Gnomes, being Palamabron's friends,
Were leagued together against Satan thro' ancient enmity.
What could Los do? How could he judge, when Satan's self believ'd
That he had not oppress'd the horses of the Harrow, nor the servants?

So Los said, "Henceforth, Palamabron, let each his own station
Keep; nor in pity false, nor in officious brotherhood, where
None needs, be active." Meantime Palamabron's horses
Rag'd with thick flames redundant, & the Harrow madden'd with fury.
Trembling Palamabron stood, the strongest of Demons trembled,
Curbing his living creatures; many of the strongest Gnomes

They bit in their wild fury, who also madden'd like wildest beasts.

Mark well my words; they are of your eternal salvation!

[PLATE 6]
Meanwhile wept Satan before Los, accusing Palamabron,
Himself exculpating with mildest speech, for himself believ'd
That he had not oppress'd nor injur'd the refractory servants.

But Satan returning to his Mills (for Palamabron had serv'd
The Mills of Satan as the easier task) found all confusion
And back return'd to Los, not fill'd with vengeance but with tears,
Himself convinc'd of Palamabron's turpitude. Los beheld
The servants of the Mills drunken with wine and dancing wild
With shouts and Palamabron's songs, rending the forests green
With ecchoing confusion, tho' the Sun was risen on high.

Then Los took off his left sandal, placing it on his head,
Signal of solemn mourning. When the servants of the Mills
Beheld the signal they in silence stood, tho' drunk with wine.
Los wept! But Rintrah also came, and Enitharmon on
His arm lean'd tremblingly, observing all these things.

And Los said. "Ye Genii of the Mills, the Sun is on high,
Your labours call you! Palamabron is also in sad dilemma:
His horses are mad, his Harrow confounded, his companions enrag'd.
Mine is the fault! I should have remember'd that pity divides the soul
And man, unmans; follow with me my Plow. This mournful day
Must be a blank in Nature; follow with me, and tomorrow again
Resume your labours, & this day shall be a mournful day."

Wildly they follow'd Los and Rintrah, & the Mills were silent,
They mourn'd all day, this mournful day of Satan & Palamabron;
And all the Elect & all the Redeem'd mourn'd one toward another

71

Upon the mountains of Albion among the cliffs of the Dead.

They Plow'd in tears! Incessant pour'd Jehovah's rain, & Molech's
Thick fires, contending with the rain, thunder'd above, rolling
Terrible over their heads. Satan wept over Palamabron.
Theotormon & Bromion contended on the side of Satan,
Pitying his youth and beauty, trembling at eternal death.
Michael contended against Satan in the rolling thunder;
Thulloh, the friend of Satan, also reprov'd him—faint their
  reproof.

But Rintrah, who is of the reprobate, of those form'd to destruction,
In indignation for Satan's soft dissimulation of friendship
Flam'd above all the plowed furrows, angry, red, and furious,
Till Michael sat down in the furrow, weary, dissolv'd in tears.
Satan, who drave the team beside him, stood angry & red;
He smote Thulloh & slew him, & he stood terrible over Michael
Urging him to arise. He wept! Enitharmon saw his tears,
But Los hid Thulloh from her sight, lest she should die of grief.
She wept; she trembled! She kissed Satan; she wept over Michael;
She form'd a Space for Satan & Michael & for the poor infected.
Trembling, she wept over the Space, & clos'd it with a tender Moon.

Los secret buried Thulloh, weeping disconsolate over the moony
  Space.

But Palamabron called down a Great Solemn Assembly,
That he who will not defend Truth, may be compelled to
Defend a Lie, that he may be snared & caught & taken.

[PLATE 7]
And all Eden descended into Palamabron's tent
Among Albion's Druids & Bards, in the caves beneath Albion's
Death Couch, in the caverns of death, in the corner of the Atlantic.

And in the midst of the Great Assembly Palamabron pray'd:
"O God protect me from my friends, that they have not power
    over me.
Thou hast giv'n me power to protect myself from my bitterest
    enemies."

Mark well my words; they are of your eternal salvation!

Then rose the Two Witnesses, Rintrah & Palamabron:
And Palamabron appeal'd to all Eden, and receiv'd
Judgment, and Lo! it fell on Rintrah and his rage,
Which now flam'd high & furious in Satan against Palamabron
Till it became a proverb in Eden: Satan is among the Reprobate.

Los in his wrath curs'd heaven & earth. He rent up Nations,
Standing on Albion's rocks among high-reared Druid temples
Which reach the stars of heaven & stretch from pole to pole.
He displac'd continents. The oceans fled before his face.
He alter'd the poles of the world, east, west & north & south,
But he clos'd up Enitharmon from the sight of all these things.

For Satan, flaming with Rintrah's fury hidden beneath his own
    mildness,
Accus'd Palamabron before the Assembly of ingratitude, of malice.
He created Seven deadly Sins, drawing out his infernal scroll
Of Moral laws and cruel punishments upon the clouds of Jehovah,
To pervert the Divine voice in its entrance to the earth;
With thunder of war & trumpets sound, with armies of disease
Punishments & deaths muster'd & number'd, saying: "I am God alone,
There is no other! Let all obey my principles of moral individuality.
I have brought them from the uppermost innermost recesses
Of my Eternal Mind; transgressors I will rend off forever,
As now I rend this accursed Family from my covering."

Thus Satan rag'd amidst the Assembly, and his bosom grew
Opake against the Divine Vision; the paved terraces of
His bosom inwards shone with fires, but the stones becoming opake
Hid him from sight, in an extreme blackness and darkness,
And there a World of deeper Ulro was open'd, in the midst
Of the Assembly, in Satan's bosom a vast unfathomable Abyss.

Astonishment held the Assembly in an awful silence, and tears
Fell down as dews of night, & a loud solemn universal groan
Was utter'd from the east & from the west & from the south
And from the north, and Satan stood opake immeasurable,
Covering the east with solid blackness, round his hidden heart,
With thunders utter'd from his hidden wheels, accusing loud
The Divine Mercy for protecting Palamabron in his tent.

Rintrah rear'd up walls of rocks and pour'd rivers & moats
Of fire round the walls; columns of fire guard around
Between Satan and Palamabron in the terrible darkness.

And Satan not having the Science of Wrath, but only of Pity,
Rent them asunder. And wrath was left to wrath, & pity to pity.
He sunk down a dreadful Death, unlike the slumbers of Beulah.

The Separation was terrible: the Dead was repos'd on his Couch
Beneath the Couch of Albion, on the seven mountains of Rome,
In the whole place of the Covering Cherub, Rome, Babylon & Tyre.
His Spectre raging furious descended into its Space.

[PLATE 8, Full-page Design]

[PLATE d, PLATE 11 in Copy D]
Then Los & Enitharmon knew that Satan is Urizen,
Drawn down by Orc & the Shadowy Female into Generation.
Oft Enitharmon enter'd weeping into the Space, there appearing

An aged Woman raving along the Streets (the Space is named
Canaan); then she return'd to Los, weary, frighted as from dreams.

The nature of a Female Space is this: it shrinks the Organs
Of Life till they become Finite & Itself seems Infinite.

And Satan vibrated in the immensity of the Space! Limited
To those without but Infinite to those within, it fell down and
Became Canaan, closing Los from Eternity in Albion's Cliffs,
A mighty Fiend against the Divine Humanity, must'ring to War.

"Satan, Ah me! is gone to his own place," said Los, "their God
I will not worship in their Churches, nor King in their Theatres.
Elynittria! whence is this Jealousy running along the mountains?
British Women were not Jealous when Greek & Roman were Jealous.
Every thing in Eternity shines by its own Internal light, but thou
Darkenest every Internal light with the arrows of thy quiver,
Bound up in the horns of Jealousy to a deadly fading Moon,
And Ocalythron binds the Sun into a Jealous Globe,
That every thing is fix'd Opake without Internal light."

So Los lamented over Satan, who triumphant divided the Nations.

[PLATE 9]
He set his face against Jerusalem to destroy the Eon of Albion.

But Los hid Enitharmon from the sight of these things
Upon the Thames, whose lulling harmony repos'd her soul,
Where Beulah lovely terminates in rocky Albion,
Terminating in Hyde Park, on Tyburn's awful brook.

And the Mills of Satan were separated into a moony Space
Among the rocks of Albion's Temples, and Satan's Druid sons
Offer the Human Victims throughout all the Earth, and Albion's

75

Dread Tomb, immortal on his Rock, overshadow'd the whole Earth,
Where Satan, making to himself Laws from his own identity,
Compell'd others to serve him in moral gratitude & submission,
Being call'd God, setting himself above all that is called God.
And all the Spectres of the Dead, calling themselves Sons of God,
In his Synagogues worship Satan under the Unutterable Name.

And it was enquir'd Why in a Great solemn Assembly
The Innocent should be condemn'd for the Guilty. Then an
      Eternal rose,

Saying: "If the Guilty should be condemn'd, he must be an
      Eternal Death,
And one must die for another throughout all Eternity.
Satan is fall'n from his station & never can be redeem'd
But must be new Created continually, moment by moment;
And therefore the Class of Satan shall be call'd the Elect, & those
Of Rintrah the Reprobate, & those of Palamabron the Redeem'd—
For he is redeem'd from Satan's Law, the wrath falling on Rintrah.
And therefore Palamabron dared not to call a solemn Assembly
Till Satan had assum'd Rintrah's wrath in the day of mourning,
In a feminine delusion of false pride, self-deciev'd."

So spoke the Eternal and confirm'd it with a thunderous oath.

But when Leutha (a Daughter of Beulah) beheld Satan's condemnation,
She down descended into the midst of the Great Solemn Assembly,
Offering herself a Ransom for Satan, taking on her his Sin.

Mark well my words; they are of your eternal salvation!

And Leutha stood glowing with varying colours immortal, heart-
      piercing,
And lovely, & her moth-like elegance shone over the Assembly.

76

At length, standing upon the golden floor of Palamabron,
She spoke: "I am the Author of this Sin; by my suggestion
My Parent power Satan has committed this transgression.
I loved Palamabron & I sought to approach his Tent,
But beautiful Elynittria with her silver arrows repell'd me,

[PLATE 10]

For her light is terrible to me; I fade before her immortal beauty.
O wherefore doth a Dragon-Form forth issue from my limbs
To sieze her new born son? Ah me! the wretched Leutha!
This to prevent, entering the doors of Satan's brain night after night
Like sweet perfumes, I stupified the masculine perceptions
And kept only the feminine awake. Hence rose his soft
Delusory love to Palamabron, admiration join'd with envy,
Cupidity unconquerable! My fault when, at noon of day,
The Horses of Palamabron call'd for rest and pleasant death,
I sprang out of the breast of Satan, over the Harrow beaming
In all my beauty, that I might unloose the flaming steeds
As Elynittria use'd to do. But too well those living creatures
Knew that I was not Elynittria, and they brake the traces.
But me the servants of the Harrow saw not but as a bow
Of varying colours on the hills; terribly rag'd the horses.
Satan astonish'd, and with power above his own controll,
Compell'd the Gnomes to curb the horses, & to throw banks of sand
Around the fiery flaming Harrow in labyrinthine forms,
And brooks between to intersect the meadows in their course.
The Harrow cast thick flames; Jehovah thunder'd above;
Chaos & ancient night fled from beneath the fiery Harrow;
The Harrow cast thick flames & orb'd us round in concave fires,
A Hell of our own making. See, its flames still gird me round.
Jehovah thunder'd above! Satan, in pride of heart,
Drove the fierce Harrow among the constellations of Jehovah,
Drawing a third part in the fires as stubble north & south
To devour Albion and Jerusalem, the Emanation of Albion,

Driving the Harrow in Pity's paths. 'Twas then, with our dark fires
Which now gird round us (O eternal torment), I form'd the Serpent
Of precious stones & gold, turn'd poisons on the sultry wastes.
The Gnomes in all that day spar'd not; they curs'd Satan bitterly.
To do unkind things in kindness! With power arm'd, to say
The most irritating things in the midst of tears and love—
These are the stings of the Serpent! Thus did we by them till thus
They in turn retaliated, and the Living Creatures madden'd.
The Gnomes labour'd. I weeping hid in Satan's inmost brain;
But when the Gnomes refus'd to labour more, with blandishments
I came forth from the head of Satan! Back the Gnomes recoil'd
And call'd me Sin, and for a sign portentous held me. Soon
Day sunk and Palamabron return'd. Trembling I hid myself
In Satan's inmost Palace of his nervous fine wrought Brain,
For Elynittria met Satan with all her singing women,
Terrific in their joy & pouring wine of wildest power.
They gave Satan their wine; indignant at the burning wrath,
Wild with prophetic fury, his former life became like a dream.
Cloth'd in the Serpent's folds, in selfish holiness demanding purity
Being most impure, self-condemn'd to eternal tears, he drove
Me from his inmost Brain, & the doors clos'd with thunder's sound.
O Divine Vision, who didst create the Female to repose
The Sleepers of Beulah, pity the repentant Leutha. My

[PLATE 11]

Sick Couch bears the dark shades of Eternal Death infolding
The Spectre of Satan; he furious refuses to repose in sleep.
I humbly bow in all my Sin before the Throne Divine.
Not so the Sick-one. Alas, what shall be done him to restore,
Who calls the Individual Law Holy, and despises the Saviour,
Glorying to involve Albion's Body in fires of eternal War?''

Now Leutha ceas'd. Tears flow'd, but the Divine Pity supported her.

78

"All is my fault. We are the Spectre of Luvah, the murderer
Of Albion. O Vala! O Luvah! O Albion! O lovely Jerusalem!
The Sin was begun in Eternity and will not rest to Eternity
Till two Eternitys meet together. Ah! lost! lost! lost! forever!"

So Leutha spoke. But when she saw that Enitharmon had
Created a New Space to protect Satan from punishment,
She fled to Enitharmon's Tent & hid herself. Loud raging
Thunder'd the Assembly dark & clouded, and they ratify'd
The kind decision of Enitharmon & gave a Time to the Space,
Even Six Thousand years, and sent Lucifer for its Guard.
But Lucifer refus'd to die & in pride he forsook his charge.
And they elected Molech, and when Molech was impatient
The Divine hand found the Two Limits; first of Opacity, then of
    Contraction.
Opacity was named Satan, Contraction was named Adam.
Triple Elohim came: Elohim wearied, fainted; they elected Shaddai.
Shaddai angry, Pahad descended; Pahad terrified, they sent Jehovah,
And Jehovah was leprous. Loud he call'd, stretching his hand to
    Eternity,
For then the Body of Death was perfected in hypocritic holiness
Around the Lamb, a Female Tabernacle woven in Cathedron's Looms.
He died as a Reprobate, he was Punish'd as a Transgressor.
Glory! Glory! Glory! to the Holy Lamb of God!
I touch the heavens as an instrument to glorify the Lord!

The Elect shall meet the Redeem'd. On Albion's rocks they shall
    meet,
Astonish'd at the Transgressor, in him beholding the Saviour.
And the Elect shall say to the Redeem'd. "We behold it is of Divine
Mercy alone, of Free Gift and Election that we live.
Our Virtues & Cruel Goodnesses have deserv'd Eternal Death."
Thus they weep upon the fatal Brook of Albion's River.

But Elynittria met Leutha in the place where she was hidden
And threw aside her arrows and laid down her sounding Bow;
She sooth'd her with soft words & brought her to Palamabron's bed
In moments new created for delusion, interwoven round about.
In dreams she bore the shadowy Spectre of Sleep & nam'd him Death.
In dreams she bore Rahab, the mother of Tirzah & her sisters,
In Lambeth's vales, in Cambridge & in Oxford, places of Thought,
Intricate labyrinths of Times and Spaces unknown that Leutha lived
In Palamabron's Tent, and Oothoon was her charming guard.

The Bard ceas'd. All consider'd, and a loud resounding murmur
Continu'd round the Halls, and much they question'd the immortal
Loud-voic'd Bard, and many condemn'd the high-toned Song,
Saying: "Pity and Love are too venerable for the imputation
Of Guilt." Others said: "If it is true, if the acts have been perform'd,
Let the Bard himself witness. Where hadst thou this terrible Song?"
The Bard replied: "I am Inspired! I know it is Truth, for I Sing

[PLATE 12]
According to the inspiration of the Poetic Genius
Who is the eternal all-protecting Divine Humanity
To whom be Glory & Power & Dominion Evermore. Amen."

Then there was great murmuring in the Heavens of Albion
Concerning Generation & the Vegetative power & concerning
The Lamb the Saviour. Albion trembled to Italy, Greece, & Egypt,
To Tartary & Hindostan & China, & to Great America,
Shaking the roots & fast foundations of the Earth in doubtfulness.
The loud voic'd bard terrify'd took refuge in Milton's bosom.

Then Milton rose up from the heavens of Albion ardorous!
The whole Assembly wept prophetic, seeing in Milton's face
And in his lineaments divine the shades of Death & Ulro.

He took off the robe of the promise & ungirded himself from the
    oath of God.

And Milton said, "I go to Eternal Death! The Nations still
Follow after the detestable Gods of Priam in pomp
Of warlike selfhood, contradicting and blaspheming.
When will the Resurrection come to deliver the sleeping body
From corruptibility? O when, Lord Jesus, wilt thou come?
Tarry no longer, for my soul lies at the gates of death.
I will arise and look forth for the morning of the grave.
I will go down to the sepulcher to see if morning breaks.
I will go down to self annihilation and eternal death,
Lest the Last Judgment come & find me unannihilate,
And I be siez'd & giv'n into the hands of my own Selfhood.
The Lamb of God is seen thro' mists & shadows, hov'ring
Over the sepulchers in clouds of Jehovah & winds of Elohim,
A disk of blood, distant, & heav'ns & earths roll dark between.
What do I here before the Judgment? Without my Emanation?
With the daughters of memory & not with the daughters of
    inspiration?
I in my Selfhood am that Satan; I am that Evil One!
He is my Spectre! In my obedience to loose him from my Hells
To claim the Hells, my Furnaces, I go to Eternal Death."

And Milton said. "I go to Eternal Death!" Eternity shudder'd,
For he took the outside course, among the graves of the dead,
A mournful shade. Eternity shudder'd at the image of eternal death.

Then on the verge of Beulah he beheld his own Shadow:
A mournful form double, hermaphroditic, male & female
In one wonderful body. And he enter'd into it
In direful pain, for the dread shadow, twenty-seven-fold
Reach'd to the depths of direst Hell, & thence to Albion's land,

Which is this earth of vegetation on which now I write.

The Seven Angels of the Presence wept over Milton's Shadow.

[PLATE 13, Full-page Design]

[PLATE 14]
As when a man dreams, he reflects not that his body sleeps,
Else he would wake; so seem'd he entering his Shadow. But
With him the Spirits of the Seven Angels of the Presence
Entering, they gave him still perceptions of his Sleeping Body,
Which now arose and walk'd with them in Eden, as an Eighth
Image Divine tho' darken'd, and tho' walking as one walks
In sleep. And the Seven comforted and supported him.

Like as a Polypus that vegetates beneath the deep
They saw his Shadow vegetated underneath the Couch
Of death. For when he enter'd into his Shadow, Himself,
His real and immortal Self, was as appear'd to those
Who dwell in immortality, as One sleeping on a couch
Of gold, and those in immortality gave forth their Emanations,
Like Females of sweet beauty, to guard round him & to feed
His lips with food of Eden in his cold and dim repose.
But to himself he seem'd a wanderer lost in dreary night.

Onwards his Shadow kept its course among the Spectres, call'd
Satan, but swift as lightning passing them. Startled the shades
Of Hell beheld him in a trail of light as of a comet
That travels into Chaos. So Milton went guarded within.

The nature of infinity is this: that every thing has its
Own Vortex, and when once a traveller thro' Eternity
Has pass'd that Vortex, he percieves it roll backward behind
His path into a globe itself infolding like a sun,

82

Or like a moon, or like a universe of starry majesty—
While he keeps onwards in his wondrous journey on the earth—
Or like a human form, a friend with whom he liv'd benevolent.
As the eye of man views both the east & west, encompassing
Its vortex, and the north & south, with all their starry host,
Also the rising sun & setting moon, he views surrounding
His corn-fields and his valleys of five hundred acres square.
Thus is the earth one infinite plane and not as apparent
To the weak traveller confin'd beneath the moony shade.
Thus is the heaven a vortex pass'd already, and the earth
A vortex not yet pass'd by the traveller thro' Eternity.

First Milton saw Albion upon the Rock of Ages,
Deadly pale outstretch'd and snowy cold, storm cover'd,
A Giant form of perfect beauty outstretch'd on the rock
In solemn death. The Sea of Time & Space thunder'd aloud
Against the rock, which was inwrapped with the weeds of death.
Hovering over the cold bosom, in its vortex Milton bent down
To the bosom of death: what was underneath soon seem'd above.
A cloudy heaven mingled with the stormy seas in loudest ruin.
But as a wintry globe descends precipitant thro' Beulah bursting
With thunders loud and terrible, so Milton's shadow fell
Precipitant loud thund'ring into the Sea of Time & Space.

Then first I saw him in the Zenith as a falling star,
Descending perpendicular, swift as the swallow or swift;
And on my left foot falling on the tarsus, enter'd there;
But from my left foot a black cloud redounding spread over Europe.

Then Milton knew that the Three Heavens of Beulah were beheld
By him on earth in his bright pilgrimage of sixty years.

[PLATE 15]
To Annihilate the Self-hood of Deceit & False Forgiveness.

83

[PLATE 16]

In those three females, whom his Wives, & those three whom his
    Daughters
Had represented and contain'd, that they might be resum'd
By giving up of Selfhood; & they distant view'd his journey
In their eternal spheres, now Human, tho' their Bodies remain clos'd
In the dark Ulro till the Judgment. Also Milton knew they and
Himself was Human, tho' now wandering thro' Death's Vale
In conflict with those Female forms, which in blood & jealousy
Surrounded him, dividing & uniting without end or number.

He saw the Cruelties of Ulro, and he wrote them down
In iron tablets; and his Wives' & Daughters' names were these:
Rahab and Tirzah, & Milcah & Malah & Noah & Hoglah.
They sat rang'd round him as the rocks of Horeb round the land
Of Canaan, and they wrote in thunder, smoke, and fire
His dictate; and his body was the Rock Sinai: that body
Which was on earth born to corruption; & the six Females
Are Hor & Peor & Bashan & Abarim & Lebanon & Hermon,
Seven rocky Masses terrible in the Desarts of Midian.

But Milton's Human Shadow continu'd journeying above
The rocky masses of the Mundane Shell in the Lands
Of Edom & Aram & Moab & Midian & Amalek.

The Mundane Shell is a vast Concave Earth, an immense
Harden'd shadow of all things upon our Vegetated Earth,
Enlarg'd into dimension & deform'd into indefinite space
In Twenty-seven Heavens and all their Hells, with Chaos
And Ancient Night, & Purgatory. It is a cavernous Earth
Of labyrinthine intricacy, twenty-seven-folds of opakeness
And finishes where the lark mounts; here Milton journeyed
In that Region call'd Midian, among the Rocks of Horeb.

For travellers from Eternity pass outward to Satan's seat,
But travellers to Eternity pass inward to Golgonooza.

Los, the Vehicular terror, beheld him, & divine Enitharmon
Call'd all her daughters, Saying: "Surely to unloose my bond
Is this Man come! Satan shall be unloos'd upon Albion."

Los heard in terror Enitharmon's words; in fibrous strength
His limbs shot forth like roots of trees against the forward path
Of Milton's journey. Urizen beheld the immortal Man,

[PLATE e, PLATE 20 in Copy D]
And Tharmas, Demon of the Waters, & Orc, who is Luvah.

The Shadowy Female seeing Milton howl'd in her lamentation
Over the Deeps, outstretching her Twenty-seven Heavens over Albion.
And thus the Shadowy Female howls in articulate howlings:

"I will lament over Milton in the lamentations of the afflicted.
My Garments shall be woven of sighs & heart broken lamentations;
The misery of unhappy Families shall be drawn out into its border,
Wrought with the needle with dire sufferings, poverty, pain & woe,
Along the rocky Island & thence throughout the whole Earth.
There shall be the sick Father & his starving Family, there
The Prisoner in the stone Dungeon & the Slave at the Mill.
I will have Writings written all over it in Human Words
That every Infant that is born upon the Earth shall read
And get by rote as a hard task of a life of sixty years.
I will have Kings inwoven upon it & Councellors & Mighty Men.
The Famine shall clasp it together with buckles & Clasps,
And the Pestilence shall be its fringe & the War its girdle,
To divide into Rahab & Tirzah that Milton may come to our tents.
For I will put on the Human Form & take the Image of God,

Even Pity & Humanity, but my Clothing shall be Cruelty.
And I will put on Holiness as a breastplate & as a helmet,
And all my ornaments shall be of the gold of broken hearts,
And the precious stones of anxiety & care & desperation & death,
And repentance for sin & sorrow & punishment & fear,
To defend me from thy terrors, O Orc, my only beloved!"

Orc, answer'd, "Take not the Human Form, O loveliest. Take not
Terror upon thee! Behold how I am & tremble lest thou also
Consume in my Consummation; but thou maist take a Form
Female & lovely, that cannot consume in Man's consummation.
Wherefore dost thou Create & Weave this Satan for a Covering?
When thou attemptest to put on the Human Form, my wrath
Burns to the top of heaven against thee in Jealousy & Fear.
Then I rend thee asunder, then I howl over thy clay & ashes.
When wilt thou put on the Female Form as in times of old,
With a Garment of Pity & Compassion like the Garment of God?
His garments are long sufferings for the Children of Men.
Jerusalem is his Garment, & not thy Covering Cherub, O lovely
Shadow of my delight, who wanderest seeking for the prey."

So spoke Orc when Oothoon & Leutha hover'd over his Couch
Of fire, in interchange of Beauty & Perfection in the darkness
Opening interiorly into Jerusalem & Babylon, shining glorious
In the Shadowy Female's bosom. Jealous her darkness grew.
Howlings fill'd all the desolate places in accusations of Sin,
In Female beauty shining in the unform'd void, & Orc in vain
Stretch'd out his hands of fire, & wooed; they triumph in his pain.

Thus darken'd the Shadowy Female tenfold, & Orc tenfold
Glow'd on his rocky Couch against the darkness; loud thunders
Told of the enormous conflict. Earthquake beneath, around,
Rent the Immortal Females, limb from limb & joint from joint,
And moved the fast foundations of the Earth to wake the Dead.

Urizen emerged from his Rocky Form & from his Snows,

[PLATE 17]

And he also darken'd his brows, freezing dark rocks between
The footsteps and infixing deep the feet in marble beds,
That Milton labour'd with his journey, & his feet bled sore
Upon the clay now chang'd to marble. Also Urizen rose
And met him on the shores of Arnon; & by the streams of the brooks.

Silent they met and silent strove among the streams, of Arnon
Even to Mahanaim, when with cold hand Urizen stoop'd down
And took up water from the river Jordan, pouring on
To Milton's brain the icy fluid from this broad cold palm.
But Milton took of the red clay of Succoth, moulding it with care
Between his palms and filling up the furrows of many years,
Beginning at the feet of Urizen, and on the bones
Creating new flesh on the Demon cold, and building him
As with new clay a Human form in the Valley of Beth Peor.

Four Universes round the Mundane Egg remain Chaotic:
One to the North, named Urthona; one to the South named Urizen;
One to the East named Luvah; one to the West named Tharmas.
They are the Four Zoas that stood around the Throne Divine!
But when Luvah assum'd the World of Urizen to the South,
And Albion was slain upon his mountains & in his tent,
All fell towards the Center in dire ruin, sinking down.
And in the South remains a burning fire, in the East a void.
In the West, a world of raging waters, in the North a solid,
Unfathomable, without end. But in the midst of these
Is built eternally the Universe of Los and Enitharmon
Towards which Milton went, but Urizen oppos'd his path.

The Man and Demon strove many periods. Rahab beheld,
Standing on Carmel; Rahab and Tirzah trembled to behold

87

The enormous strife, one giving life, the other giving death
To his adversary. And they sent forth all their sons & daughters
In all their beauty to entice Milton across the river.

The Twofold form Hermaphroditic and the Double-sexed,
The Female-male & the Male-female, self-dividing stood
Before him in their beauty & in cruelties of holiness,
Shining in darkness, glorious upon the deeps of Entuthon,
Saying: "Come thou to Ephraim! Behold the Kings of Canaan!
The beautiful Amalekites! Behold the fires of youth
Bound with the Chain of Jealousy by Los & Enitharmon!
The banks of Cam, cold learning's streams, London's dark-frowning
        towers
Lament upon the winds of Europe in Rephaim's Vale,
Because Ahania rent apart into a desolate night,
Laments, & Enion wanders like a weeping inarticulate voice,
And Vala labours for her bread & water among the Furnaces.
Therefore bright Tirzah triumphs, putting on all beauty
And all perfection in her cruel sports among the Victims.
Come, bring with thee Jerusalem with songs on the Grecian Lyre!
In Natural Religion, in experiments on Men,
Let her be Offer'd up to Holiness! Tirzah numbers her;
She numbers with her fingers every fibre ere it grow.
Where is the Lamb of God? Where is the promise of his coming?
Her shadowy Sisters form the bones, even the bones of Horeb
Around the marrow, and the orbed scull around the brain.
His images are born for War! For Sacrifice to Tirzah!
To Natural Religion! To Tirzah the Daughter of Rahab the Holy!
She ties the knot of nervous fibres into a white brain!
She ties the knot of bloody veins into a red hot heart!
Within her bosom Albion lies embalm'd, never to awake.
Hand is become a rock; Sinai & Horeb is Hyle & Coban;
Scofield is bound in iron armour before Reuben's Gate!
She ties the knot of milky seed into two lovely Heavens,

[PLATE 18]

Two yet but one, each in the other sweet reflected! These
Are our Three Heavens beneath the shades of Beulah, land of rest.
Come then to Ephraim & Manasseh, O beloved-one!
Come to my ivory palaces, O beloved of thy mother,
And let us bind thee in the bands of War & be thou King
Of Canaan and reign in Hazor where the Twelve Tribes meet."

So spoke they as in one voice. Silent Milton stood before
The darken'd Urizen, as the sculptor silent stands before
His forming image: he walks round it patient labouring.
Thus Milton stood forming bright Urizen, while his Mortal part
Sat frozen in the rock of Horeb, and his Redeemed portion
Thus form'd the Clay of Urizen, but within that portion
His real Human walk'd above in power and majesty
Tho' darken'd, and the Seven Angels of the Presence attended him.

O how can I, with my gross tongue that cleaveth to the dust,
Tell of the Four-fold Man, in starry numbers fitly order'd?
Or how can I with my cold hand of clay? But thou, O Lord,
Do with me as thou wilt, for I am nothing, and vanity.
If thou choose to elect a worm, it shall remove the mountains.
For that portion nam'd the Elect, the Spectrous body of Milton,
Redounding from my left foot into Los's Mundane space,
Brooded over his Body in Horeb against the Resurrection,
Preparing it for the Great Consummation; red the Cherub on Sinai
Glow'd, but in terrors folded round his clouds of blood.

Now Albion's sleeping Humanity began to turn upon his Couch,
Feeling the electric flame of Milton's awful precipitate descent.
Seest thou the little winged fly, smaller than a grain of sand?
It has a heart like thee, a brain open to heaven & hell.
Withinside wondrous & expansive, its gates are not clos'd.
I hope thine are not. Hence it clothes itself in rich array.

Hence thou art cloth'd with human beauty, O thou mortal man.
Seek not thy heavenly father then beyond the skies;
There Chaos dwells & ancient Night, & Og & Anak old,
For every human heart has gates of brass & bars of adamant,
Which few dare unbar because dread Og & Anak guard the gates
Terrific! And each mortal brain is wall'd and moated round
Within: and Og & Anak watch here; here is the Seat
Of Satan in its Webs. For in brain and heart and loins
Gates open behind Satan's Seat to the City of Golgonooza,
Which is the spiritual fourfold London, in the loins of Albion.

Thus Milton fell thro' Albion's heart, travelling outside of Humanity
Beyond the Stars in Chaos, in Caverns of the Mundane Shell.

But many of the Eternals rose up from the eternal tables
Drunk with the Spirit, burning round the Couch of death they stood,
Looking down into Beulah, wrathful, fill'd with rage.
They rend the heavens round the Watchers in a fiery circle
And round the Shadowy Eighth. The Eight close up the Couch
Into a tabernacle and flee with cries down to the Deeps,
Where Los opens his three wide gates, surrounded by raging fires.
They soon find their own place & join the Watchers of the Ulro.

Los saw them and a cold pale horror cover'd o'er his limbs.
Pondering, he knew that Rintrah & Palamabron might depart,
Even as Reuben & as Gad, gave up himself to tears.
He sat down on his anvil-stock and lean'd upon the trough,
Looking into the black water, mingling it with tears.

At last when desperation almost tore his heart in twain
He recollected an old Prophecy, in Eden recorded
And often sung to the loud harp at the immortal feasts,
That Milton of the Land of Albion should up ascend
Forwards from Ulro from the Vale of Felpham and set free

Orc from his Chain of Jealousy; he started at the thought

[PLATE 19]

And down descended into Udan-Adan; it was night,
And Satan sat sleeping upon his Couch in Udan-Adan.
His Spectre slept, his Shadow woke (when one sleeps th'other wakes).

But Milton entering my Foot, I saw in the nether
Regions of Imagination, also all men on Earth
And all in Heaven saw in the nether regions of the Imagination,
In Ulro beneath Beulah, the vast breach of Milton's descent.
But I knew not that it was Milton, for man cannot know
What passes in his members till periods of Space & Time
Reveal the secrets of Eternity; for more extensive
Than any other earthly things are Man's earthly lineaments.
And all this Vegetable World appear'd on my left Foot
As a bright sandal form'd immortal of precious stones & gold:
I stooped down & bound it on to walk forward thro' Eternity.

There is in Eden a sweet River, of milk & liquid pearl,
Nam'd Ololon, on whose mild banks dwelt those who Milton drove
Down into Ulro. And they wept in long resounding song
For seven days of eternity, and the river's living banks,
The mountains, wail'd, & every plant that grew in solemn sighs
    lamented.

When Luvah's bulls each morning drag the sulphur Sun out of the
    Deep,
Harness'd with starry harness, black & shining, kept by black slaves
That work all night at the starry harness, strong and vigorous
They drag the unwilling Orb. At this time all the Family
Of Eden heard the lamentation, and Providence began.
But when the clarions of day sounded, they drown'd the lamentations,
And when night came all was silent in Ololon, & all refus'd to lament

In the still night, fearing lest they should others molest.

Seven mornings Los heard them, as the poor bird within the shell
Hears its impatient parent bird, and Enitharmon heard them,
But saw them not, for the blue Mundane Shell inclos'd them in.

And they lamented that they had in wrath & fury & fire
Driven Milton into the Ulro, for now they knew too late
That it was Milton the Awakener. They had not heard the Bard,
Whose song call'd Milton to the attempt. And Los heard these
       laments.
He heard them call in prayer all the Divine Family,
And he beheld the Cloud of Milton stretching over Europe.

But all the Family Divine collected as Four Suns
In the Four Points of heaven, East, West & North & South,
Enlarging and enlarging till their Disks approach'd each other,
And when they touch'd closed together Southward in One Sun
Over Ololon. And as One Man, who weeps over his brother
In a dark tomb, so all the Family Divine wept over Ololon,
Saying: "Milton goes to Eternal Death!" So saying they groan'd
       in spirit
And were troubled; and again the Divine Family groaned in spirit.

And Ololon said, "Let us descend also, and let us give
Ourselves to death in Ulro among the Transgressors.
Is Virtue A Punisher? O no! How is this wondrous thing,
This World beneath, unseen before, this refuge from the wars
Of Great Eternity, unnatural refuge, unknown by us till now?
Or are these the pangs of repentance? Let us enter into them."

Then the Divine Family said, "Six Thousand Years are now
Accomplish'd in this World of Sorrow; Milton's Angel knew
The Universal Dictate; and you also feel this Dictate.

And now you know this World of Sorrow and feel Pity. Obey
The Dictate. Watch over this World and with your brooding wings
Renew it to Eternal Life. Lo! I am with you alway.
But you cannot renew Milton. He goes to Eternal Death."

So spoke the Family Divine as One Man even Jesus,
Uniting in One with Ololon, & the appearance of One Man,
Jesus the Saviour, appear'd coming in the Clouds of Ololon:

[PLATE 20]
Tho' driven away with the Seven Starry Ones into the Ulro,
Yet the Divine Vision remains Every-where For-ever. Amen.
And Ololon lamented for Milton with a great lamentation.

While Los heard indistinct in fear, what time I bound my sandals
On to walk forward thro' Eternity, Los descended to me
And Los behind me stood, a terrible flaming Sun, just close
Behind my back. I turned round in terror, and behold!
Los stood in that fierce glowing fire, & he also stoop'd down
And bound my sandals on in Udan Adan; trembling I stood
Exceedingly with fear & terror, standing in the Vale
Of Lambeth, but he kissed me and wish'd me health.
And I became One Man with him arising in my strength.
'Twas too late now to recede. Los had enter'd into my soul:
His terrors now possess'd me whole! I arose in fury & strength.

"I am that Shadowy Prophet who Six Thousand Years ago
Fell from my station in the Eternal bosom. Six Thousand Years
Are finish'd. I return! Both Time & Space obey my will.
I in Six Thousand years walk up and down, for not one Moment
Of Time is lost, nor one Event of Space unpermanent.
But all remain. Every fabric of Six Thousand Years
Remains permanent, tho' on the Earth where Satan
Fell and was cut off, all things vanish & are seen no more.

They vanish not from me & mine; we guard them first & last.
The generations of men run on in the tide of Time
But leave their destin'd lineaments permanent forever & ever."
So spoke Los as we went along to his supreme abode.

Rintrah and Palamabron met us at the Gate of Golgonooza,
Clouded with discontent, & brooding in their minds terrible things.

They said: "O Father most beloved! O merciful Parent,
Pitying and permitting evil, tho' strong & mighty to destroy.
Whence is this Shadow terrible? Wherefore dost thou refuse
To throw him into the Furnaces? Knowest thou not that he
Will unchain Orc & let loose Satan, Og, Sihon & Anak
Upon the Body of Albion? For this he is come. Behold it written
Upon his fibrous left Foot black, most dismal to our eyes.
The Shadowy Female shudders thro' heaven in torment inexpressible,
And all the Daughters of Los prophetic wail; yet in deceit,
They weave a new Religion from new Jealousy of Theotormon.
Milton's Religion is the cause; there is no end to destruction!
Seeing the Churches at their Period in terror & despair,
Rahab created Voltaire, Tirzah created Rousseau,
Asserting the Self-righteousness against the Universal Saviour,
Mocking the Confessors & Martyrs, claiming Self-righteousness
With cruel Virtue, making War upon the Lamb's Redeemed
To perpetuate War & Glory, to perpetuate the Laws of Sin.
They perverted Swedenborg's Visions in Beulah & in Ulro
To destroy Jerusalem as a Harlot & her Sons as Reprobates,
To raise up Mystery the Virgin Harlot, Mother of War,
Babylon the Great, the Abomination of Desolation!
O Swedenborg, strongest of men, the Samson shorn by the Churches,
Shewing the Transgressors in Hell, the proud Warriors in Heaven,
Heaven as a Punisher & Hell as One under Punishment,
With Laws from Plato & his Greeks to renew the Trojan Gods
In Albion, & to deny the value of the Saviour's blood.

But then I rais'd up Whitefield, Palamabron rais'd up Wesley.
And these are the cries of the Churches before the two Witnesses'
Faith in God, the dear Saviour, who took on the likeness of men,
Becoming obedient to death, even the death of the Cross.
'The Witnesses lie dead in the Street of the Great City;
No Faith is in all the Earth; the Book of God is trodden under Foot.
He sent his two Servants, Whitefield & Wesley. Were they Prophets?
Or were they Idiots or Madmen? Shew us Miracles!'

[PLATE 21, Full-page Design]

[PLATE 22]

Can you have greater Miracles than these? Men who devote
Their life's whole comfort to intire scorn & injury & death?
Awake, thou sleeper on the Rock of Eternity. Albion, Awake!
The trumpet of Judgment hath twice sounded; all Nations are awake,
But thou art still heavy and dull. Awake, Albion, awake!
Lo, Orc arises on the Atlantic. Lo, his blood and fire
Glow on America's shore. Albion turns upon his Couch;
He listens to the sounds of War, astonish'd and confounded.
He weeps into the Atlantic deep, yet still in dismal dreams
Unawaken'd, and the Covering Cherub advances from the East.
How long shall we lay dead in the Street of the great City?
How long beneath the Covering Cherub give our Emanations?
Milton will utterly consume us & thee, our beloved Father.
He hath enter'd into the Covering Cherub, becoming one with
Albion's dread Sons; Hand, Hyle & Coban surround him as
A girdle; Gwendolen & Conwenna as a garment woven
Of War & Religion. Let us descend & bring him chained
To Bowlahoola, O father most beloved! O mild Parent!
Cruel in thy mildness, pitying and permitting evil
Tho' strong and mighty to destroy, O Los our beloved Father!"

Like the black storm, coming out of Chaos beyond the stars,

95

It issues thro' the dark & intricate caves of the Mundane Shell,
Passing the planetary visions, & the well adorned Firmament.
The Sun rolls into Chaos & the Stars into the Desarts,
And then the storms become visible, audible, & terrible,
Covering the light of day, & rolling down upon the mountains,
Deluge all the country round. Such is a vision of Los
When Rintrah & Palamabron spoke, and such his stormy face
Appear'd, as does the face of heaven when cover'd with thick storms,
Pitying and loving, tho' in frowns of terrible perturbation.

But Los dispers'd the clouds even as the strong winds of Jehovah.
And Los thus spoke: "O Noble Sons, be patient yet a little.
I have embrac'd the falling Death; he is become One with me.
Oh Sons, we live not by wrath, by mercy alone we live!
I recollect an old Prophecy in Eden recorded in gold, and oft
Sung to the harp: that Milton of the land of Albion
Should up ascend forward from Felpham's Vale & break the Chain
Of Jealousy from all its roots. Be patient therefore, O my Sons.
These lovely Females form sweet night and silence and secret
Obscurities to hide from Satan's Watch-Fiends Human loves
And graces, lest they write them in their Books, & in the Scroll
Of mortal life, to condemn the accused who, at Satan's Bar,
Tremble in Spectrous Bodies continually day and night,
While on the Earth they live in sorrowful Vegetations.
O when shall we tread our Wine-presses in heaven and Reap
Our wheat with shoutings of joy, and leave the Earth in peace?
Remember how Calvin and Luther in fury premature
Sow'd War and stern division between Papists & Protestants.
Let it not be so now! O go not forth in Martyrdoms & Wars!
We were plac'd here by the Universal Brotherhood & Mercy
With powers fitted to circumscribe this dark Satanic death,
And that the Seven Eyes of God may have space for Redemption.
But how this is as yet we know not, and we cannot know
Till Albion is arisen; then, patient, wait a little while.

Six Thousand years are pass'd away, the end approaches fast;
This mighty one is come from Eden; he is of the Elect
Who died from Earth & is return'd before the Judgment. This thing
Was never known, that one of the holy dead should willing return.
Then, patient, wait a little while till the Last Vintage is over,
Till we have quench'd the Sun of Salah in the Lake of Udan Adan.
O my dear Sons! leave not your Father, as your brethren left me.
Twelve Sons successive fled away in that thousand years of sorrow,

[PLATE 23]
Of Palamabron's Harrow, & of Rintrah's wrath & fury.
Reuben & Manazzoth & Gad & Simeon & Levi
And Ephraim & Judah were Generated because
They left me, wandering with Tirzah. Enitharmon wept
One thousand years, and all the Earth was in a wat'ry deluge.
We called him Menassheh because of the Generations of Tirzah,
Because of Satan; & the Seven Eyes of God continually
Guard round them, but I, the Fourth Zoa, am also set
The Watchman of Eternity; the Three are not, & I am preserved.
Still my four mighty ones are left to me in Golgonooza:
Still Rintrah fierce, and Palamabron mild & piteous,
Theotormon fill'd with care, Bromion loving Science.
You, O my Sons, still guard round Los. O wander not & leave me.
Rintrah, thou will rememberest when Amalek & Canaan
Fled with their Sister Moab into that abhorred Void.
They became Nations in our sight beneath the hands of Tirzah.
And Palamabron, thou rememberest when Joseph, an infant
Stolen from his nurse's cradle wrap'd in needle-work
Of emblematic texture, was sold to the Amalekite,
Who carried him down into Egypt, where Ephraim & Menassheh
Gather'd my Sons together in the Sands of Midian.
And if you also flee away and leave your Father's side,
Following Milton into Ulro, altho' your power is great,
Surely you also shall become poor mortal vegetations

Beneath the Moon of Ulro. Pity then your Father's tears.
When Jesus rais'd Lazarus from the Grave, I stood & saw
Lazarus, who is the Vehicular Body of Albion the Redeem'd,
Arise into the Covering Cherub, who is the Spectre of Albion,
By martyrdoms to suffer, to watch over the Sleeping Body
Upon his Rock beneath his Tomb. I saw the Covering Cherub
Divide Four-fold into Four Churches when Lazarus arose:
Paul, Constantine, Charlemaine, Luther. Behold they stand before us
Stretch'd over Europe & Asia. Come, O Sons, come, come away!
Arise, O Sons, give all your strength against Eternal Death
Lest we are vegetated, for Cathedron's Looms weave only Death,
A Web of Death; & were it not for Bowlahoola & Allamanda
No Human Form, but only a Fibrous Vegetation,
A Polypus of soft affections without Thought or Vision
Must tremble in the Heavens & Earths thro' all the Ulro space.
Throw all the Vegetated Mortals into Bowlahoola.
But as to this Elected Form who is return'd again,
He is the Signal that the Last Vintage now approaches,
Nor Vegetation may go till the earth is reap'd."

So Los spoke. Furious they descended to Bowlahoola & Allamanda,
Indignant, unconvinc'd by Los's arguments & thunders rolling.
They saw that wrath now sway'd and now pity absorb'd him.
As it was, so it remain'd & no hope of an end.

Bowlahoola is nam'd Law by mortals; Tharmas founded it,
Because of Satan, before Luban in the City of Golgonooza.
But Golgonooza is nam'd Art & Manufacture by mortal men.

In Bowlahoola Los's Anvils stand & his Furnaces rage;
Thundering the Hammers beat & the Bellows blow loud,
Living, self-moving, mourning, lamenting, & howling incessantly.
Bowlahoola thro' all its porches feels, tho' too fast founded,
Its pillars & porticoes to tremble at the force

Of mortal or immortal arm; and softly lilling flutes
Accordant with the horrid labours make sweet melody.
The Bellows are the Animal Lungs; the Hammers the Animal Heart;
The Furnaces the Stomach for digestion—terrible their fury.
Thousands & thousands labour, thousands play on instruments,
Stringed or fluted, to ameliorate the sorrows of slavery.
Loud sport the dancers in the dance of death, rejoicing in carnage.
The hard dentant Hammers are lull'd by the flutes' lula lula.
The bellowing Furnaces blare by the long sounding clarion.
The double drum drowns howls & groans; the shrill fife shrieks &
    cries;
The crooked horn mellows the hoarse raving serpent, terrible but
    harmonious.
Bowlahoola is the Stomach in every individual man.

Los is by mortals nam'd Time, Enitharmon is nam'd Space.
But they depict him bald & aged who is in eternal youth
All powerful, and his locks flourish like the brows of morning.
He is the Spirit of Prophecy, the ever apparent Elias.
Time is the mercy of Eternity; without Time's swiftness
Which is the swiftest of all things, all were eternal torment.
All the Gods of the Kingdoms of Earth labour in Los's Halls.
Every one is a fallen Son of the Spirit of Prophecy.
He is the Fourth Zoa, that stood around the Throne Divine.

[PLATE 24]
But the Wine-press of Los is eastward of Golgonooza, before
    the Seat
Of Satan, Luvah laid the foundation & Urizen finish'd it in
    howling woe.
How red the sons & daughters of Luvah! Here they tread the grapes;
Laughing & shouting, drunk with odours, many fall o'erwearied.
Drown'd in the wind is many a youth & maiden. Those around
Lay them on skins of Tygers & of the spotted Leopard & the Wild Ass

Till they revive, or bury them in cool grots, making lamentation.

This Wine-press is call'd War on Earth; it is the Printing-Press
Of Los, and here he lays his words in order above the mortal brain,
As cogs are form'd in a wheel to turn the cogs of the adverse wheel.

Timbrels & violins sport round the Wine-presses; the little Seed,
The sportive Root, The Earth-worm, the gold Beetle, the wise Emmet
Dance round the Wine-presses of Luvah; the centipede is there,
The ground Spider with many eyes, the Mole clothed in velvet,
The Ambitious Spider in his sullen web, the lucky golden Spinner,
The Earwig arm'd, the tender Maggot, emblem of immortality,
The Flea, Louse, Bug, the Tape-Worm, all the Armies of Disease,
Visible or invisible to the slothful vegetating Man.
The slow Slug, the Grasshopper that sings & laughs & drinks—
Winter comes, he folds his slender bones without a murmur.
The cruel Scorpion is there, the Gnat, Wasp, Hornet & the Honey
     Bee,
The Toad & venomous Newt, the Serpent cloth'd in gems & gold.
They throw off their gorgeous raiment; they rejoice with loud jubilee
Around the Wine-presses of Luvah, naked & drunk with wine.

There is the Nettle that stings with soft down, and there
The indignant Thistle, whose bitterness is bred in his milk,
Who feeds on contempt of his neighbour, there all the idle Weeds
That creep around the obscure places shew their various limbs,
Naked in all their beauty dancing round the Wine-presses.

But in the Wine-presses the Human Grapes sing not, nor dance.
They howl & writhe in shoals of torment, in fierce flames consuming.
In chains of iron & in dungeons circled with ceaseless fires,
In pits & dens & shades of death, in shapes of torment & woe:
The plates & screws & wracks & saws & cords & fires & cisterns,
The cruel joys of Luvah's Daughters lacerating with knives

And whips their Victims, & the deadly sport of Luvah's Sons.

They dance around the dying, & they drink the howl & groan.
They catch the shrieks in cups of gold; they hand them to one another.
These are the sports of love, & these the sweet delights of
      amorous play,
Tears of the grape, the death sweat of the cluster, the last sigh
Of the mild youth who listens to the lureing songs of Luvah.

But Allamanda, call'd on Earth Commerce, is the Cultivated Land
Around the City of Golgonooza in the Forests of Entuthon.
Here the Sons of Los labour against Death Eternal, through all
The Twenty-seven Heavens of Beulah in Ulro, Seat of Satan,
Which is the False Tongue beneath Beulah; it is the Sense of Touch.
The Plow goes forth in tempests & lightnings & the Harrow cruel
In blights of the east; the heavy Roller follows in howlings of woe.

Urizen's sons here labour also, & here are seen the Mills
Of Theotormon, on the verge of the Lake of Udan-Adan.
These are the starry voids of night & the depths & caverns of earth.
These Mills are oceans, clouds & waters ungovernable in their fury.
Here are the stars created & the seeds of all things planted.
And here the Sun & Moon recieve their fixed destinations.

But in Eternity the Four Arts: Poetry, Painting, Music,
And Architecture which is Science are the Four Faces of Man.
Not so in Time & Space; there, Three are shut out, and only
Science remains thro' Mercy; & by means of Science the Three
Become apparent in Time & Space in the Three Professions,

That Man may live upon Earth till the time of his awaking.
And from these Three, Science derives every Occupation of Men.
And Science is Divided into Bowlahoola & Allamanda.

[PLATE 25]

Loud shout the Sons of Luvah at the Wine-presses, as Los descended
With Rintrah & Palamabron in his fires of resistless fury.

The Wine-press on the Rhine groans loud, but all its central beams
Act more terrific in the central Cities of the Nations
Where Human Thought is crush'd beneath the iron hand of Power.
There Los puts all into the Press, the Oppressor & the Oppressed
Together, ripe for the Harvest & Vintage & ready for the Loom.

They sang at the Vintage, "This is the Last Vintage, & Seed
Shall no more be sown upon Earth till all the Vintage is over
And all gather'd in, till the Plow has pass'd over the Nations
And the Harrow & heavy thundering Roller upon the mountains."

And loud the Souls howl round the Porches of Golgonooza,
Crying, "O God deliver us to the Heavens or to the Earths,
That we may preach righteousness & punish the sinner with death."
But Los refused, till all the Vintage of Earth was gather'd in.

And Los stood & cried to the Labourers of the Vintage in voice of awe:
"Fellow Labourers! The Great Vintage & Harvest is now upon Earth.
The whole extent of the Globe is explored. Every scatter'd Atom
Of Human Intellect now is flocking to the sound of the Trumpet.
All the Wisdom which was hidden in caves & dens, from ancient
Time, is now sought out from Animal & Vegetable & Mineral.
The Awakener is come, outstretch'd over Europe. The Vision of God
   is fulfilled.
The Ancient Man upon the Rock of Albion Awakes.
He listens to the sounds of War astonish'd & ashamed.
He sees his Children mock at Faith and deny Providence.
Therefore you must bind the Sheaves not by Nations or Families;
You shall bind them in Three Classes; according to their Classes
So shall you bind them, Separating What has been Mixed

Since Men began to be Wove into Nations by Rahab & Tirzah,
Since Albion's Death & Satan's Cutting off from our awful Fields.
When, under pretence to benevolence, the Elect Subdu'd All
From the Foundation of the World. The Elect is one Class. You
Shall bind them separate. They cannot Believe in Eternal Life
Except by Miracle & a New Birth. The other two Classes
The Reprobate who never cease to Believe and the Redeem'd,
Who live in doubts & fears perpetually tormented by the Elect—
These you shall bind in a twin-bundle for the Consummation.
But the Elect must be saved fires of Eternal Death
To be formed into the Churches of Beulah that they destroy not
    the Earth.
For in every Nation & every Family the Three Classes are born,
And in every Species of Earth, Metal, Tree, Fish, Bird, & Beast.
We form the Mundane Egg, that Spectres, coming by fury or amity
All is the same, & every one remains in his own energy.
Go forth, Reapers, with rejoicing. You sowed in tears,
But the time of your refreshing cometh. Only a little moment
Still abstain from pleasure & rest, in the labours of eternity,
And you shall Reap the whole Earth from Pole to Pole, from Sea
    to Sea,
Beginning at Jerusalem's Inner Court, Lambeth, ruin'd and given
To the detestable Gods of Priam, to Apollo, and at the Asylum
Given to Hercules, who labour in Tirzah's Looms for bread,
Who set Pleasure against Duty, who Create Olympic crowns
To make Learning a burden & the Work of the Holy Spirit Strife,
The Thor & cruel Odin who first rear'd the Polar Caves.
Lambeth mourns calling Jerusalem; she weeps & looks abroad
For the Lord's coming, that Jerusalem may overspread all Nations.
Crave not for the mortal & perishing delights, but leave them
To the weak, and pity the weak as your infant care. Break not
Forth in your wrath, lest you also are vegetated by Tirzah.
Wait till the Judgement is past, till the Creation is consumed
And then rush forward with me into the glorious spiritual

Vegetation: the Supper of the Lamb & his Bride, and the
Awaking of Albion our friend and ancient companion."

So Los spoke. But lightnings of discontent broke on all sides round
And murmurs of thunder rolling heavy, long & loud over the
    mountains,
While Los call'd his Sons around him to the Harvest & the Vintage.

Thou seest the Constellations in the deep & wondrous Night;
They rise in order and continue their immortal courses
Upon the mountains & in vales with harp & heavenly song,
With flute & clarion, with cups & measures fill'd with foaming wine.
Glitt'ring the streams reflect the Vision of beatitude,
And the calm Ocean joys beneath & smooths his awful waves.

[PLATE 26]
These are the Sons of Los, & these the Labourers of the Vintage.
Thou seest the gorgeous clothed Flies that dance & sport in summer
Upon the sunny brooks & meadows; every one the dance
Knows in its intricate mazes of delight artful to weave,
Each one to sound his instruments of music in the dance,
To touch each other & recede, to cross & change & return.
These are the Children of Los. Thou seest the Trees on mountains:
The wind blows heavy, loud they thunder thro' the darksom sky,
Uttering prophecies & speaking instructive words to the sons
Of men. These are the Sons of Los! These the Visions of Eternity.
But we see only as it were the hem of their garments
When with our vegetable eyes we view these wond'rous Visions.

There are Two Gates thro' which all Souls descend: One Southward
From Dover Cliff to Lizard Point, the other toward the North—
Caithness & rocky Durness, Pentland & John Groat's House.

The Souls descending to the Body wail on the right hand

Of Los, & those deliver'd from the Body on the left hand.
For Los against the east his force continually bends
Along the Valleys of Middlesex, from Hounslow to Blackheath,
Lest those Three Heavens of Beulah should the Creation destroy,
And lest they should descend before the north & south Gates.
Groaning with pity, he among the wailing Souls laments.

And these the Labours of the Sons of Los in Allamanda,
And in the City of Golgonooza, & in Luban & around
The Lake of Udan-Adan, in the Forests of Entuthon Benython
Where Souls incessant wail, being piteous Passions & desires
With neither lineament nor form, but like to wat'ry clouds.
The Passions & Desires descend upon the hungry winds,
For such alone Sleepers remain meer passion & appetite.
The Sons of Los clothe them & feed & provide houses & fields.

And every Generated Body in its inward form
Is a garden of delight & a building of magnificence,
Built by the Sons of Los in Bowlahoola & Allamanda,
And the herbs & flowers & furnature & beds & chambers
Continually woven in the Looms of Enitharmon's Daughters,
In bright Cathedron's golden Dome with care & love & tears.
For the various Classes of Men are all mark'd out determinate
In Bowlahoola &, as the Spectres choose their affinities,
So they are born on Earth, & every Class is determinate
But not by Natural but by Spiritual power alone, because
The Natural power continually seeks & tends to Destruction
Ending in Death, which would of itself be Eternal Death.
And all are Class'd by Spiritual & not by Natural power.

And every Natural Effect has a Spiritual Cause and Not
A Natural, for a Natural Cause only seems: it is a Delusion
Of Ulro, & a ratio of the perishing Vegetable Memory.

[PLATE 27]

Some Sons of Los surround the Passions with porches of iron & silver,
Creating form & beauty around the dark regions of sorrow,
Giving to airy nothing a name and a habitation
Delightful: with bounds to the Infinite putting off the Indefinite
Into most holy forms of Thought: (such is the power of inspiration).
They labour incessant, with many tears & afflictions,
Creating the beautiful House for the piteous sufferer.

Others Cabinets richly fabricate of gold & Ivory,
For Doubts & fears unform'd & wretched & melancholy.
The little weeping Spectre stands on the threshold of Death
Eternal; and sometimes two Spectres like lamps quivering,
And often malignant, they combat (heart-breaking, sorrowful &
    piteous).
Antamon takes them into his beautiful flexible hands
As the Sower takes the seed, or as the Artist his clay
Or fine wax, to mould artful a model for golden ornaments.
The soft hands of Antamon draw the indelible line,
Form immortal with golden pen, such as the Spectre admiring
Puts on the sweet form; then smiles Antamon bright thro' his
    windows.
The Daughters of beauty look up from their Loom & prepare
The integument soft for its clothing with joy & delight.

But Theotormon & Sotha stand in the Gate of Luban anxious.
Their numbers are seven million & seven thousand & seven hundred.
They contend with the weak Spectres; they fabricate soothing forms.
The Spectre refuses, he seeks cruelty. They create the crested Cock.
Terrified the Spectre screams & rushes in fear into their Net
Of kindness & compassion & is born a weeping terror.
Or they create the Lion & Tyger in compassionate thunderings.
Howling the Spectres flee; they take refuge in Human lineaments.

The Sons of Ozoth within the Optic Nerve stand fiery glowing.
And the number of his sons is eight millions & eight.
They give delights to the man unknown, artificial riches
They give to scorn, & their possessors to trouble & sorrow & care,
Shutting the sun, & moon, & stars, & trees, & clouds, & waters,
And hills out from the Optic Nerve & hardening it into a bone
Opake, and like the black pebble on the enraged beach,
While the poor indigent is like the diamond which, tho' cloth'd
In rugged covering in the mine, is open all within,
And in his hallow'd center holds the heavens of bright eternity.
Ozoth here builds walls of rocks against the surging sea,
And timbers crampt with iron cramps bar in the joys of life
From fell destruction in the Spectrous cunning or rage. He Creates
The speckled Newt, the Spider & Beetle, the Rat & Mouse,
The Badger & Fox; they worship before his feet in trembling fear.

But others of the Sons of Los build Moments & Minutes & Hours
And Days & Months & Years & Ages & Periods, wondrous buildings.
And every Moment has a Couch of gold for soft repose.
(A Moment equals a pulsation of the artery.)
And between every two Moments stands a Daughter of Beulah
To feed the Sleepers on their Couches with maternal care.
And every Minute has an azure Tent with silken Veils,
And every Hour has a bright golden Gate carved with skill,
And every Day & Night has Walls of brass & Gates of adamant,
Shining like precious stones & ornamented with appropriate signs,
And every Month, a silver paved Terrace builded high,
And every Year, invulnerable Barriers with high Towers.
And every Age is Moated deep with Bridges of silver & gold,
And every Seven Ages is Incircled with a Flaming Fire.
Now Seven Ages is amounting to Two Hundred Years.
Each has its Guard, each Moment, Minute, Hour, Day, Month,
     & Year;
All are the work of Fairy hands of the Four Elements;

The Guard are Angels of Providence on duty evermore.
Every Time Less than a pulsation of the artery
Is equal in its period & value to Six Thousand Years,

[PLATE 28]
For in this Period the Poet's Work is Done, and all the Great
Events of Time start forth & are conciev'd in such a Period,
Within a Moment, a Pulsation of the Artery.

The sky is an immortal Tent built by the Sons of Los,
And every Space that a Man views around his dwelling-place,
Standing on his own roof, or in his garden on a mount
Of twenty-five cubits in height, such space is his Universe;
And on its verge the Sun rises & sets, the Clouds bow
To meet the flat Earth & the Sea in such an order'd Space,
The Starry heavens reach no further, but here bend and set
On all sides, & the two Poles turn on their valves of gold.
And if he move his dwelling-place, his heavens also move
Where'er he goes, & all his neighbourhood bewail his loss.
Such are the Spaces called Earth & such its dimension.
As to that false appearance which appears to the reasoner
As of a Globe rolling thro' Voidness, it is a delusion of Ulro.
The Microscope knows not of this nor the Telescope; they alter
The ratio of the Spectator's Organs but leave Objects untouch'd.
For every Space larger than a red Globule of Man's blood
Is visionary, and is created by the Hammer of Los.
And every Space smaller than a Globule of Man's blood opens
Into Eternity of which this vegetable Earth is but a shadow.
The red Globule is the unwearied Sun by Los created
To measure Time and Space to mortal Men every morning.
Bowlahoola & Allamanda are placed on each side
Of that Pulsation & that Globule; terrible their power.

But Rintrah & Palamabron govern over Day & Night

108

In Allamanda & Entuthon Benython where Souls wail,
Where Orc incessant howls, burning in fires of Eternal Youth,
Within the vegetated mortal Nerves; for every Man born is joined
Within into One mighty Polypus, and this Polypus is Orc.

But in the Optic vegetative Nerves Sleep was transformed
To Death in old time by Satan, the father of Sin & Death.
And Satan is the Spectre of Orc, & Orc is the generate Luvah.

But in the Nerves of the Nostrils, Accident being Formed
Into Substance & Principle, by the cruelties of Demonstration
It became Opake & Indefinite. But the Divine Saviour,
Formed it into a Solid by Los's Mathematic power.
He named the Opake, Satan; he named the Solid, Adam.

And in the Nerves of the Ear (for the Nerves of the Tongue are closed)
On Albion's Rock Los stands, creating the glorious Sun each morning;
And when unwearied, in the evening, he creates the Moon,
Death to delude, who all in terror at their splendor leaves
His prey, while Los appoints, & Rintrah & Palamabron guide
The Souls clear from the Rock of Death, that Death himself may
     wake
In his appointed season when the ends of heaven meet.

Then Los conducts the Spirits to be Vegetated into
Great Golgonooza, free from the four iron pillars of Satan's Throne—
Temperance, Prudence, Justice, Fortitude, the four pillars of tyranny—
That Satan's Watch Fiends touch them not before they Vegetate.

But Enitharmon and her Daughters take the pleasant charge,
To give them to their lovely heavens till the Great Judgment Day.
Such is their lovely charge. But Rahab & Tirzah pervert
Their mild influences. Therefore the Seven Eyes of God walk round
The Three Heavens of Ulro, where Tirzah & her Sisters

Weave the black Woof of Death upon Entuthon Benython,
In the Vale of Surrey where Horeb terminates in Rephaim.
The stamping feet of Zelophehad's Daughters are cover'd with
    Human gore
Upon the treadles of the Loom; they sing to the winged shuttle.
The River rises above his banks to wash the Woof;
He takes it in his arms, he passes it in strength thro' his current.
The veil of human miseries is woven over the Ocean
From the Atlantic to the Great South Sea, the Erythrean.

Such is the World of Los, the labour of six thousand years.
Thus Nature is a Vision of the Science of the Elohim.

End of the First Book

[PLATE 29, Full-page Design]

[PLATE 30]
How wide the Gulf & Unpassable! between Simplicity & Insipidity

MILTON

Contraries are Positives
A Negation is not a Contrary

Book the Second

There is a place where Contrarieties are equally True.
This place is called Beulah. It is a pleasant lovely Shadow
Where no dispute can come, because of those who Sleep.
Into this place the Sons & Daughters of Ololon descended
With solemn mourning, into Beulah's moony shades & hills,
Weeping for Milton; mute wonder held the Daughters of Beulah,
Enraptur'd with affection sweet and mild benevolence.

Beulah is evermore Created around Eternity, appearing
To the Inhabitants of Eden around them on all sides.
But Beulah to its Inhabitants appears within each district
As the beloved infant in his mother's bosom round incircled
With arms of love & pity & sweet compassion. But to
The Sons of Eden the moony habitations of Beulah
Are from Great Eternity a mild & a pleasant Rest.

And it is thus Created. Lo, the Eternal Great Humanity,
To whom be Glory & Dominion Evermore, Amen,
Walks among all his awful Family, seen in every face
As the breath of the Almighty. Such are the Words of man to man
In the great Wars of Eternity, in fury of Poetic Inspiration
To build the Universe stupendous: Mental forms Creating.

But the Emanations trembled exceedingly, nor could they
Live, because the life of Man was too exceeding unbounded.

His joy became terrible to them; they trembled & wept,
Crying with one voice, "Give us a habitation & a place
In which we may be hidden under the shadow of wings.
For if we, who are but for a time & who pass away in winter,
Behold these wonders of Eternity, we shall consume;
But you, O our Fathers & Brothers, remain in Eternity.
But grant us a Temporal Habitation; do you speak
To us, we will obey your words as you obey Jesus
The Eternal who is blessed for ever & ever. Amen."

So spoke the lovely Emanations, & there appear'd a pleasant
Mild Shadow above, beneath, & on all sides round.

[PLATE 31]
Into this pleasant Shadow all the weak & weary,
Like Women & Children, were taken away as on wings
Of dovelike softness, & shadowy habitations prepared for them.
But every Man return'd & went, still going forward thro'
The Bosom of the Father in Eternity on Eternity;
Neither did any lack or fall into Error without
A Shadow to repose in all the Days of happy Eternity.

Into this pleasant Shadow, Beulah, all Ololon descended.
And when the Daughters of Beulah heard the lamentation,
All Beulah wept, for they saw the Lord coming in the Clouds.
And the Shadows of Beulah terminate in rocky Albion.

And all Nations wept in affliction, Family by Family:
Germany wept towards France & Italy; England wept & trembled
Towards America; India rose up from his golden bed,
As one awaken'd in the night. They saw the Lord coming
In the Clouds of Ololon with Power & Great Glory!
And all the Living Creatures of the Four Elements wail'd
With bitter wailing: these in the aggregate are named Satan

And Rahab, they know not of Regeneration, but only of Generation;
The Fairies, Nymphs, Gnomes & Genii of the Four Elements,
Unforgiving & unalterable, these cannot be Regenerated
But must be Created, for they know only of Generation.
These are the Gods of the Kingdoms of the Earth, in contrarious
And cruel opposition, Element against Element, opposed in War
Not Mental as the Wars of Eternity, but a Corporeal Strife.
In Los's Halls continual labouring in the Furnaces of Golgonooza;
Orc howls on the Atlantic; Enitharmon trembles; All Beulah weeps.

Thou hearest the Nightingale begin the Song of Spring.
The Lark sitting upon his earthy bed, just as the morn
Appears, Listens silent, then springing from the waving Corn-field!
    Loud
He leads the Choir of Day: trill, trill, trill, trill.
Mounting upon the wings of light into the Great Expanse,
Reecchoing against the lovely blue & shining heavenly Shell,
His little throat labours with inspiration; every feather
On throat & breast & wings vibrates with the effluence Divine.
All Nature listens silent to him & the awful Sun
Stands still upon the mountain looking on this little Bird
With eyes of soft humility, & wonder, love, & awe.
Then loud from their green covert all the Birds begin their Song.
The Thrush, the Linnet & the Goldfinch, Robin & the Wren
Awake the Sun from his sweet reverie upon the Mountain;
The Nightingale again assays his song & thro' the day
And thro' the night warbles luxuriant, every Bird of Song
Attending his loud harmony with admiration & love.
This is a Vision of the lamentation of Beulah over Ololon.

Thou percievest the Flowers put forth their precious Odours,
And none can tell how from so small a center comes such sweets,
Forgetting that within that Center Eternity expands
Its ever during doors, that Og & Anak fiercely guard.

113

First, e'er the morning breaks, joy opens in the flowery bosoms,
Joy even to tears, which the Sun rising dries; first the Wild Thyme
And Meadow-sweet, downy & soft waving among the reeds,
Light springing on the air, lead the sweet Dance; they wake
The Honeysuckle sleeping on the Oak; the flaunting beauty
Revels along upon the wind; the White-thorn, lovely May,
Opens her many lovely eyes; listening, the Rose still sleeps,
None dare to wake her; soon she bursts her crimson curtain'd bed
And comes forth in the majesty of beauty; every Flower—
The Pink, the Jessamine, the Wall-flower, the Carnation
The Jonquil, the mild Lilly—opes her heavens. Every Tree
And Flower & Herb soon fill the air with an innumerable Dance,
Yet all in order sweet & lovely. Men are sick with Love!
Such is a Vision of the lamentation of Beulah over Ololon.

[PLATE f, PLATE 35 in Copy D]
And Milton oft sat up on the Couch of Death & oft conversed
In vision & dream beatific with the Seven Angels of the Presence.

"I have turned my back upon these Heavens builded on cruelty.
My Spectre still wandering thro' them follows my Emanation.
He hunts her footsteps thro' the snow & the wintry hail & rain.
The idiot Reasoner laughs at the Man of Imagination,
And from laughter proceeds to murder by undervaluing calumny."

Then Hillel, who is Lucifer, replied over the Couch of Death,
And thus the Seven Angels instructed him & thus they converse.

"We are not Individuals but States, Combinations of Individuals.
We were Angels of the Divine Presence, & were Druids in Annandale,
Compell'd to combine into Form by Satan, the Spectre of Albion,
Who made himself a God & destroyed the Human Form Divine.
But the Divine Humanity & Mercy gave us a Human Form, כדבים
as multitudes
Because we were combin'd in Freedom & holy Brotherhood, Vox Populi

114

While those combin'd by Satan's Tyranny first in the blood of War
And Sacrifice, & next in Chains of imprisonment are Shapeless Rocks,
Retaining only Satan's Mathematic Holiness, Length, Bredth &
    Highth,
Calling the Human Imagination, which is the Divine Vision &
    Fruition
In which Man liveth eternally, madness & blasphemy, against
Its own Qualities, which are Servants of Humanity, not Gods or Lords.
Distinguish therefore States from Individuals in those States.
States Change, but Individual Identities never change nor cease.
You cannot go to Eternal Death in that which can never Die.
Satan & Adam are States Created into Twenty-seven Churches.
And thou, O Milton, art a State about to be Created,
Called Eternal Annihilation, that none but the Living shall
Dare to enter, & they shall enter triumphant over Death
And Hell & the Grave, States that are not, but ah! Seem to be.

Judge then of thy Own Self, thy Eternal Lineaments explore.
What is Eternal & what Changeable? & what Annihilable?
The Imagination is not a State; it is the Human Existence itself.
Affection or Love becomes a State, when divided from Imagination.
The Memory is a State always, & the Reason is a State
Created to be Annihilated & a new Ratio Created.
Whatever can be Created can be Annihilated; Forms cannot.
The Oak is cut down by the Ax, the Lamb falls by the Knife,
But their Forms Eternal Exist For-ever. Amen. Hallelujah."

Thus they converse with the Dead, watching round the Couch
    of Death.
For God himself enters Death's Door always with those that enter,
And lays down in the Grave with them in Visions of Eternity,
Till they awake & see Jesus & the Linen Clothes lying,
That the Females had Woven for them, & the Gates of their
    Father's House.

[PLATE 32]
And the Divine Voice was heard in the Songs of Beulah Saying:

"When I first Married you, I gave you all my whole Soul.
I thought that you would love my loves & joy in my delights,
Seeking for pleasures in my pleasures, O daughter of Babylon.
Then thou wast lovely, mild & gentle; now thou art terrible
In jealousy, & unlovely in my sight, because thou hast cruelly
Cut off my loves in fury, till I have no love left for thee.
Thy love depends on him thou lovest, & on his dear loves
Depend thy pleasures, which thou hast cut off by jealousy.
Therefore I shew my Jealousy & set before you Death.
Behold Milton descended to Redeem the Female Shade
From Death Eternal; such your lot, to be continually Redeem'd
By death & misery of those you love & by Annihilation.
When the Sixfold Female percieves that Milton annihilates
Himself, that seeing all his loves by her cut off, he leaves
Her also, intirely abstracting himself from Female loves,
She shall relent in fear of death; She shall begin to give
Her maidens to her husband, delighting in his delight.
And then & then alone begins the happy Female joy
As it is done in Beulah, & thou, O Virgin Babylon, Mother of
      Whoredoms,
Shalt bring Jerusalem in thine arms in the night watches and,
No longer turning her a wandering Harlot in the streets,
Shalt give her into the arms of God your Lord & Husband."

Such are the Songs of Beulah in the Lamentations of Ololon.

[PLATE 33, Full-page Design]

[PLATE 34]
And all the Songs of Beulah sounded comfortable notes
To comfort Ololon's lamentation, for they said,

"Are you the Fiery Circle that late drove in fury & fire
The Eight Immortal Starry-Ones down into Ulro dark,
Rending the Heavens of Beulah with your thunders & lightnings?
And can you thus lament & can you pity & forgive?
Is terror chang'd to pity? O wonder of Eternity!"

And the Four States of Humanity in its Repose
Were shewed them. First of Beulah, a most pleasant Sleep
On Couches soft, with mild music, tended by Flowers of Beulah,
Sweet Female forms, winged or floating in the air spontaneous.
The Second State is Alla, & the third State Al-Ulro;
But the Fourth State is dreadful; it is named Or-Ulro.
The First State is in the Head, the Second is in the Heart,
The Third in the Loins & Seminal Vessels, & the Fourth
In the Stomach & Intestines, terrible, deadly, unutterable.
And he whose Gates are open'd in those Regions of his Body
Can from those Gates view all these wonderous Imaginations.

But Ololon sought the Or-Ulro & its fiery Gates
And the Couches of the Martyrs, & many Daughters of Beulah
Accompany them down to the Ulro with soft melodious tears,
A long journey & dark thro' Chaos in the track of Milton's course,
To where the Contraries of Beulah War beneath Negation's Banner.

Then view'd from Milton's Track they see the Ulro: a vast Polypus
Of living fibres down into the Sea of Time & Space growing,
A self-devouring monstrous Human Death Twenty-Seven fold.
Within it sit Five Females & the nameless Shadowy Mother,
Spinning it from their bowels with songs of amorous delight
And melting cadences that lure the Sleepers of Beulah down
The River Storge (which is Arnon) into the Dead Sea.
Around this Polypus Los continual builds the Mundane Shell.

Four Universes round the Universe of Los remain Chaotic,

Four intersecting Globes, & the Egg form'd World of Los
In midst, stretching from Zenith to Nadir, in midst of Chaos.
One of these Ruin'd Universes is to the North, named Urthona;
One in the South—this was the glorious World of Urizen;
One to the East, of Luvah; one to the West, of Tharmas.
But when Luvah assumed the World of Urizen in the South,
All fell towards the Center, sinking downward in dire Ruin.

Here in these Chaoses the Sons of Ololon took their abode,
In Chasms of the Mundane Shell which open on all sides round,
Southward & by the East within the Breach of Milton's descent
To watch the time, pitying & gentle to waken Urizen.
They stood in a dark land of death, of fiery corroding waters,
Where lie in evil death the Four Immortals pale and cold,
And the Eternal Man, even Albion, upon the Rock of Ages.
Seeing Milton's Shadow some Daughters of Beulah trembling
Return'd, but Ololon remain'd before the Gates of the Dead.

And Ololon looked down into the Heavens of Ulro in fear.
They said, "How are the Wars of Man, which in Great Eternity
Appear around in the External Spheres of Visionary Life,
Here render'd Deadly within the Life & Interior Vision!
How are the Beasts & Birds & Fishes, & Plants & Minerals
Here fix'd into a frozen bulk, subject to decay & death!
Those Visions of Human Life & Shadows of Wisdom & Knowledge

[PLATE 35]
Are here frozen to unexpansive deadly destroying terrors,
And War & Hunting, the Two Fountains of the River of Life,
Are become Fountains of bitter Death & of corroding Hell,
Till Brotherhood is chang'd into a Curse & a Flattery
By Differences between Ideas, that ideas themselves (which are
The Divine Members) may be slain in offerings for sin.
O dreadful Loom of Death! O piteous Female forms compell'd

To weave the Woof of Death! On Camberwell Tirzah's Courts,
Malah's on Blackheath, Rahab & Noah dwell on Windsor's heights;
Where once the Cherubs of Jerusalem spread to Lambeth's Vale
Milcah's Pillars shine from Harrow to Hampstead, where Hoglah,
On Highgate's heights magnificent, Weaves over trembling Thames
To Shooters' Hill and thence to Blackheath, the dark Woof. Loud,
Loud roll the Weights & Spindles over the whole Earth, let down
On all sides round to the Four Quarters of the World, eastward on
Europe to Euphrates & Hindu, to Nile & back, in Clouds
Of Death across the Atlantic to America North & South."

So spoke Ololon in reminiscence astonish'd, but they
Could not behold Golgonooza without passing the Polypus,
A wondrous journey not passable by Immortal feet, & none
But the Divine Saviour can pass it without annihilation.
For Golgonooza cannot be seen till, having pass'd the Polypus,
It is viewed on all sides round by a Four-fold Vision,
Or till you become Mortal & Vegetable in Sexuality,
Then you behold its mighty Spires & Domes of ivory & gold.

And Ololon examined all the Couches of the Dead,
Even of Los & Enitharmon, & all the Sons of Albion
And his Four Zoas, terrified & on the verge of Death.
In midst of these was Milton's Couch, & when they saw Eight
Immortal Starry-Ones, guarding the Couch in flaming fires,
They thunderous utter'd all a universal groan, falling down
Prostrate before the Starry Eight, asking with tears forgiveness,
Confessing their crime with humiliation and sorrow.

O how the Starry Eight rejoic'd to see Ololon descended,
And now that a wide road was open to Eternity
By Ololon's descent thro' Beulah to Los & Enitharmon.
For mighty were the multitudes of Ololon, vast the extent
Of their great sway reaching from Ulro to Eternity,

Surrounding the Mundane Shell outside in its Caverns
And through Beulah, and all silent forbore to contend
With Ololon, for they saw the Lord in the Clouds of Ololon.

There is a Moment in each Day that Satan cannot find,
Nor can his Watch Fiends find it, but the Industrious find
This Moment & it multiply; & when it once is found,
It renovates every Moment of the Day if rightly placed.
In this Moment Ololon descended to Los & Enitharmon,
Unseen beyond the Mundane Shell Southward in Milton's track.

Just in this Moment when the morning odours rise abroad,
And first from the Wild Thyme, stands a Fountain in a rock
Of crystal flowing into two Streams: one flows thro' Golgonooza
And thro' Beulah to Eden beneath Los's western Wall,
The other flows thro' the Aerial Void & all the Churches,
Meeting again in Golgonooza beyond Satan's Seat.

The Wild Thyme is Los's Messenger to Eden, a mighty Demon—
Terrible, deadly & poisonous his presence in Ulro dark—
Therefore he appears only a small Root creeping in grass,
Covering over the Rock of Odours his bright purple mantle
Beside the Fount, above the Lark's Nest in Golgonooza.
Luvah slept here in death, & here is Luvah's empty Tomb.
Ololon sat beside this Fountain on the Rock of Odours.

Just at the place to where the Lark mounts is a Crystal Gate.
It is the entrance of the First Heaven named Luther: for
The Lark is Los's Messenger thro' the Twenty-seven Churches,
That the Seven Eyes of God who walk even to Satan's Seat,
Thro' all the Twenty-seven Heavens, may not slumber nor sleep.
But the Lark's Nest is at the Gate of Los, at the eastern
Gate of wide Golgonooza, & the Lark is Los's Messenger.

[PLATE 36]

When on the highest lift of his light pinions he arrives
At that bright Gate, another Lark meets him, & back to back
They touch their pinions, tip tip, and each descend
To their respective Earths, & there all night consult with Angels
Of Providence & with the Eyes of God all night in slumbers
Inspired, & at the dawn of day send out another Lark
Into another Heaven to carry news upon his wings.
Thus are the Messengers dispatch'd till they reach the Earth again
In the East Gate of Golgonooza, & the Twenty-eighth bright
Lark met the Female Ololon descending into my Garden.
Thus it appears to Mortal eyes & those of the Ulro Heavens,
But not thus to Immortals: the Lark is a mighty Angel.

For Ololon step'd into the Polypus within the Mundane Shell.
They could not step into Vegetable Worlds without becoming
The enemies of Humanity, except in a Female Form.
And as One Female, Ololon and all its mighty Hosts
Appear'd, a Virgin of twelve years. Nor time nor space was
To the perception of the Virgin Ololon, but as the
Flash of lightning, but more quick, the Virgin in my Garden
Before my Cottage stood, for the Satanic Space is delusion.

For when Los join'd with me he took me in his fi'ry whirlwind:
My Vegetated portion was hurried from Lambeth's shades,
He set me down in Felpham's Vale & prepar'd a beautiful
Cottage for me that in three years I might write all these Visions
To display Nature's cruel holiness, the deceits of Natural Religion.
Walking in my Cottage Garden, sudden I beheld
The Virgin Ololon & address'd her as a Daughter of Beulah,
"Virgin of Providence, fear not to enter into my Cottage.
What is thy message to thy friend? What am I now to do?
Is it again to plunge into deeper affliction? Behold me
Ready to obey, but pity thou my Shadow of Delight.

Enter My Cottage, comfort her, for she is sick with fatigue."

[PLATE 37]
The Virgin answer'd, "Knowest thou of Milton who descended
Driven from Eternity? Him I seek, terrified at my Act
In Great Eternity which thou knowest! I come him to seek."

So Ololon utter'd in words distinct the anxious thought.
Mild was the voice, but more distinct than any earthly,
That Milton's Shadow heard, & condensing all his Fibres
Into a strength impregnable of majesty & beauty infinite,
I saw he was the Covering Cherub & within him Satan
And Rahab, in an outside which is fallacious, within
Beyond the outline of identity, in the Selfhood deadly.
And he appear'd the Wicker Man of Scandinavia, in whom
Jerusalem's children consume in flames among the Stars.

Descending down into my Garden, a Human Wonder of God
Reaching from heaven to earth, a Cloud & Human Form,
I beheld Milton with astonishment & in him beheld
The Monstrous Churches of Beulah, the Gods of Ulro dark,
Twelve monstrous dishumaniz'd terrors, Synagogues of Satan,
A Double Twelve & Thrice Nine: such their divisions.

And these their Names & their Places within the Mundane Shell:
In Tyre & Sidon I saw Baal & Ashtaroth; in Moab Chemosh;
In Ammon Molech, loud his Furnaces rage among the Wheels
Of Og, a pealing loud the cries of the Victims of Fire,
And pale his Priestesses infolded in Veils of Pestilence, border'd
With War, Woven in Looms of Tyre & Sidon by beautiful Ashtaroth;
In Palestine Dagon, Sea Monster, worship'd o'er the Sea;
Thammuz in Lebanon & Rimmon in Damascus curtain'd;
Osiris, Isis, Orus in Egypt, dark their Tabernacles on Nile,
Floating with solemn songs, & on the Lakes of Egypt nightly

With pomp, even till morning break & Osiris appear in the sky;
But Belial of Sodom & Gommorah, obscure Demon of Bribes
And secret Assasinations, not worship'd nor ador'd, but
With the finger on the lips & the back turn'd to the light;
And Saturn, Jove & Rhea of the Isles of the Sea remote.
These Twelve Gods are the Twelve Spectre Sons of the Druid Albion.

And these the Names of the Twenty-seven Heavens & their Churches:
Adam, Seth, Enos, Cainan, Mahalaleel, Jared, Enoch,
Methuselah, Lamech. These are Giants mighty, Hermaphroditic.
Noah, Shem, Arphaxad, Cainan the second, Salah, Heber,
Peleg, Reu, Serug, Nahor, Terah: these are the Female-Males,
A Male within a Female hid as in an Arc & Curtains;
Abraham, Moses, Solomon, Paul, Constantine, Charlemaine,
Luther: these seven are the Male-Females, the Dragon Forms,
Religion hid in War, a Dragon red & hidden Harlot.

All these are seen in Milton's Shadow, who is the Covering Cherub,
The Spectre of Albion in which the Spectre of Luvah inhabits
In the Newtonian Voids between the Substances of Creation.

For the Chaotic Voids outside of the Stars are measured by
The Stars, which are the boundaries of Kingdoms, Provinces,
And Empires of Chaos invisible to the Vegetable Man.
The Kingdom of Og is in Orion; Sihon is in Ophiucus.
Og has Twenty-seven Districts; Sihon's Districts Twenty-one.
From Star to Star, Mountains & Valleys, terrible dimension
Stretch'd out compose the Mundane Shell, a mighty Incrustation
Of Forty-eight deformed Human Wonders of the Almighty,
With Caverns whose remotest bottoms meet again beyond
The Mundane Shell in Golgonooza, but the Fires of Los rage
In the remotest bottoms of the Caves, that none can pass
Into Eternity that way, but all descend to Los,
To Bowlahoola & Allamanda & to Entuthon Benython.

The Heavens are the Cherub, the Twelve Gods are Satan,

[PLATE 38, Full-page Design]

[PLATE 39]

And the Forty-eight Starry Regions are Cities of the Levites,
The Heads of the Great Polypus, Four-fold twelve enormity,
In mighty & mysterious comingling, enemy with enemy,
Woven by Urizen into Sexes from his mantle of years.
And Milton, collecting all his fibres into impregnable strength,
Descended down a Paved work of all kinds of precious stones
Out from the eastern sky, descending down into my Cottage
Garden, clothed in black, severe & silent he descended.

The Spectre of Satan stood upon the roaring sea & beheld
Milton within his sleeping Humanity; trembling & shudd'ring
He stood upon the waves, a Twenty-seven-fold mighty Demon
Gorgeous & beautiful; loud roll his thunders against Milton;
Loud Satan thunder'd, loud & dark upon mild Felpham shore,
Not daring to touch one fibre he howl'd round upon the Sea.

I also stood in Satan's bosom & beheld its desolations!
A ruin'd Man, a ruin'd building of God not made with hands;
Its plains of burning sand; its mountains of marble terrible;
Its pits & declivities flowing with molten ore & fountains
Of pitch & nitre; its ruin'd palaces & cities & mighty works;
Its furnaces of affliction in which his Angels & Emanations
Labour with blacken'd visages among its stupendous ruins;
Arches & pyramids & porches, colonades & domes,
In which dwells Mystery Babylon; here is her secret place
From hence she comes forth on the Churches in delight;
Here is her Cup fill'd with its poisons in these horrid vales,
And here her scarlet Veil woven in pestilence & war;
Here is Jerusalem bound in chains, in the Dens of Babylon.

In the Eastern porch of Satan's Universe Milton stood & said:
"Satan! my Spectre! I know my power thee to annihilate
And be a greater in thy place, & be thy Tabernacle,
A covering for thee to do thy will, till one greater comes
And smites me as I smote thee & becomes my covering.
Such are the Laws of thy false Heav'ns; but Laws of Eternity
Are not such; know thou, I come to Self Annihilation.
Such are the Laws of Eternity that each shall mutually
Annihilate himself for others' good, as I for thee.
Thy purpose & the purpose of thy Priests & of thy Churches
Is to impress on men the fear of death, to teach
Trembling & fear, terror, constriction, abject selfishness.
Mine is to teach Men to despise death & to go on
In fearless majesty annihilating Self, laughing to scorn
Thy Laws & terrors, shaking down thy Synagogues as webs.
I come to discover before Heav'n & Hell the Self righteousness
In all its Hypocritic turpitude, opening to every eye
These wonders of Satan's holiness, shewing to the Earth
The Idol Virtues of the Natural Heart, & Satan's Seat
Explore in all its Selfish Natural Virtue & put off
In Self annihilation all that is not of God alone,
To put off Self & all I have, ever & ever. Amen."

Satan heard, Coming in a cloud with trumpets & a flaming fire
Saying: "I am God the judge of all, the living & the dead
Fall therefore down & worship me; submit thy supreme
Dictate to my eternal Will, & to my dictate bow.
I hold the Balances of Right & Just & mine the Sword.
Seven Angels bear my Name & in those Seven I appear.
But I alone am God & I alone in Heav'n & Earth
Of all that live dare utter this, others tremble & bow,

[PLATE 40]
Till All Things become One Great Satan, in Holiness

125

Oppos'd to Mercy, and the Divine Delusion, Jesus, be no more."

Suddenly around Milton on my Path, the Starry Seven
Burn'd terrible! My Path became a solid fire, as bright
As the clear Sun, & Milton silent came down on my Path.
And there went forth from the Starry limbs of the Seven, Forms
Human, with Trumpets innumerable, sounding articulate
As the Seven spake; and they stood in a mighty Column of Fire
Surrounding Felpham's Vale, reaching to the Mundane Shell, Saying,
"Awake, Albion, awake! reclaim thy Reasoning Spectre. Subdue
Him to the Divine Mercy. Cast him down into the Lake
Of Los, that ever burneth with fire, ever & ever, Amen!
Let the Four Zoas awake from Slumbers of Six Thousand Years."

Then loud the Furnaces of Los were heard & seen as Seven Heavens,
Stretching from south to north over the mountains of Albion.

Satan heard; trembling round his Body, he incircled it.
He trembled with exceeding great trembling & astonishment,
Howling in his Spectre round his Body, hung'ring to devour,
But fearing for the pain, for if he touches a Vital,
His torment is unendurable; therefore he cannot devour,
But howls round it as a lion round his prey continually.
Loud Satan thunder'd, loud & dark upon mild Felpham's Shore,
Coming in a Cloud with Trumpets & with Fiery Flame,
An awful Form eastward from midst of a bright Paved-work
Of precious stones, by Cherubim surrounded, so permitted
(Lest he should fall apart in his Eternal Death) to imitate
The Eternal Great Humanity Divine surrounded by
His Cherubim & Seraphim in ever happy Eternity.
Beneath sat Chaos: Sin on his right hand, Death on his left,
And Ancient Night spread over all the heav'n his Mantle of Laws.
He trembled with exceeding great trembling & astonishment.

Then Albion rose up in the Night of Beulah on his Couch
Of dread repose seen by the visionary eye; his face is toward
The east, toward Jerusalem's Gates; groaning he sat above
His rocks. London & Bath & Legions & Edinburgh
Are the four pillars of his Throne: his left foot near London
Covers the shades of Tyburn; his instep from Windsor
To Primrose Hill, stretching to Highgate & Holloway;
London is between his knees, its basements fourfold;
His right foot stretches to the sea on Dover cliffs, his heel
On Canterbury's ruins; his right hand covers lofty Wales,
His left Scotland; his bosom girt with gold involves
York, Edinburgh, Durham & Carlisle & on the front
Bath, Oxford, Cambridge, Norwich; his right elbow
Leans on the Rocks of Erin's Land, Ireland, ancient nation;
His head bends over London; he sees his embodied Spectre
Trembling before him with exceeding great trembling & fear.
He views Jerusalem & Babylon, his tears flow down.
He mov'd his right foot to Cornwall, his left to the Rocks of Bognor.
He strove to rise to walk into the Deep but, strength failing,
Forbad & down with dreadful groans he sunk upon his Couch
In moony Beulah. Los, his strong Guard, walks round beneath the
    Moon.

Urizen faints in terror, striving among the Brooks of Arnon
With Milton's Spirit, as the Plowman or Artificer or Shepherd,
While in the labours of his Calling, sends his Thought abroad
To labour in the ocean or in the starry heaven. So Milton
Labour'd in Chasms of the Mundane Shell; tho' here before
My Cottage midst the Starry Seven, where the Virgin Ololon
Stood trembling in the Porch, loud Satan thunder'd on the stormy Sea,
Circling Albion's Cliffs in which the Four-fold World resides,
Tho' seen in fallacy outside, a fallacy of Satan's Churches.

[PLATE 41, Full-page Design]

127

[PLATE 42]

Before Ololon Milton stood & perciev'd the Eternal Form
Of that mild Vision; wondrous were their acts by me unknown
Except remotely, and I heard Ololon say to Milton:

"I see thee strive upon the Brooks of Arnon; there a dread
And awful Man I see, o'ercover'd with the mantle of years.
I behold Los & Urizen, I behold Orc & Tharmas,
The Four Zoas of Albion, & thy Spirit with them striving,
In Self annihilation giving thy life to thy enemies.
Are those who contemn Religion & seek to annihilate it
Become in their Feminine portions the causes & promoters
Of these Religions? How is this thing, this Newtonian Phantasm,
This Voltaire & Rousseau, this Hume & Gibbon & Bolingbroke,
This Natural Religion, this impossible absurdity?
Is Ololon the cause of this? O where shall I hide my face?
These tears fall for the little-ones, the Children of Jerusalem,
Lest they be annihilated in thy annihilation."

No sooner she had spoke but Rahab Babylon appear'd
Eastward upon the Paved work across Europe & Asia,
Glorious as the midday Sun in Satan's Bosom glowing,
A Female hidden in a Male, Religion hidden in War
Nam'd Moral Virtue, cruel two-fold Monster shining bright,
A Dragon red & hidden Harlot which John in Patmos saw.

And all beneath the Nations innumerable of Ulro
Appear'd: the Seven Kingdoms of Canaan & Five Baalim
Of Philistea, into Twelve divided, call'd after the Names
Of Israel, as they are in Eden, Mountain, River & Plain,
City & sandy Desart intermingled beyond mortal ken.

But turning toward Ololon in terrible majesty Milton
Replied: "Obey thou the Words of the Inspired Man.

All that can be, can be annihilated, must be annihilated
That the Children of Jerusalem may be saved from slavery.
There is a Negation, & there is a Contrary.
The Negation must be destroy'd to redeem the Contraries.
The Negation is the Spectre, the Reasoning Power in Man.
This is a false Body, an Incrustation over my Immortal
Spirit, a Selfhood, which must be put off & annihilated alway.
To cleanse the Face of my Spirit by Self-examination;

[PLATE 43]
To bathe in the Waters of Life, to wash off the Not Human;
I come in Self-annihilation & the grandeur of Inspiration:
To cast off Rational Demonstration by Faith in the Saviour;
To cast off the rotten rags of Memory by Inspiration;
To cast off Bacon, Locke & Newton from Albion's covering;
To take off his filthy garments, & clothe him with Imagination;
To cast aside from Poetry all that is not Inspiration,
That it no longer shall dare to mock with the aspersion of Madness
Cast on the Inspired by the tame high finisher of paltry Blots,
Indefinite, or paltry Rhymes, or paltry Harmonies,
Who creeps into State Government like a catterpiller to destroy;
To cast off the idiot Questioner who is always questioning
But never capable of answering, who sits with a sly grin
Silent plotting when to question, like a thief in a cave,
Who publishes doubt & calls it knowledge, whose Science is Despair,
Whose pretence to knowledge is Envy, whose whole Science is
To destroy the Wisdom of Ages to gratify ravenous Envy
That rages round him like a Wolf day & night without rest.
He smiles with condescension; he talks of Benevolence & Virtue,
And those who act with Benevolence & Virtue they murder time on
        time.
These are the destroyers of Jerusalem, these are the murderers
Of Jesus, who deny the Faith & mock at Eternal Life,
Who pretend to Poetry that they may destroy Imagination

By imitation of Nature's Images drawn from Remembrance.
These are the Sexual Garments, the Abomination of Desolation,
Hiding the Human Lineaments as with an Ark & Curtains
Which Jesus rent, & now shall wholly purge away with Fire
Till Generation is swallow'd up in Regeneration."

Then trembled the Virgin Ololon & reply'd in clouds of despair:
"Is this our Feminine Portion, the Six-fold Miltonic Female?
Terribly this Portion trembles before thee, O awful Man.
Altho' our Human Power can sustain the severe contentions
Of Friendship, our Sexual cannot, but flies into the Ulro.
Hence arose all our terrors in Eternity, & now remembrance
Returns upon us. Are we Contraries, O Milton, Thou & I?
O Immortal! how were we led to War the Wars of Death?
Is this the Void Outside of Existence, which if enter'd into

[PLATE 44]
Becomes a Womb? & is this the Death Couch of Albion?
Thou goest to Eternal Death & all must go with thee."

So saying, the Virgin divided Six-fold, & with a shriek
Dolorous that ran thro' all Creation, a Double Six-fold Wonder,
Away from Ololon she divided & fled into the depths
Of Milton's Shadow, as a Dove upon the stormy Sea.

Then as a Moony Ark Ololon descended to Felpham's Vale
In clouds of blood, in streams of gore, with dreadful thunderings
Into the Fires of Intellect that rejoic'd in Felpham's Vale
Around the Starry Eight; with one accord the Starry Eight became
One Man, Jesus the Saviour, wonderful! Round his limbs
The Clouds of Ololon folded, as a Garment dipped in blood,
Written within & without in woven letters, & the Writing
Is the Divine Revelation in the Litteral expression,
A Garment of War. I heard it nam'd the Woof of Six Thousand Years.

And I beheld the Twenty-four Cities of Albion
Arise upon their Thrones to Judge the Nations of the Earth,
And the Immortal Four in whom the Twenty-four appear Four-fold
Arose around Albion's body. Jesus wept & walked forth
From Felpham's Vale clothed in Clouds of blood, to enter into
Albion's Bosom, the bosom of death, & the Four surrounded him
In the Column of Fire in Felpham's Vale; then to their mouths the
    Four
Applied their Four Trumpets & them sounded to the Four winds.

Terror struck in the Vale, I stood at that immortal sound,
My bones trembled. I fell outstretch'd upon the path
A moment, & my Soul return'd into its mortal state,
To Resurrection & Judgment in the Vegetable Body,
And my sweet Shadow of Delight stood trembling by my side.

Immediately the Lark mounted with a loud trill from Felpham's Vale,
And the Wild Thyme from Wimbleton's green & impurpled Hills,
And Los & Enitharmon rose over the Hills of Surrey.
Their clouds roll over London with a south wind; soft Oothoon
Pants in the Vales of Lambeth, weeping o'er her Human Harvest.
Los listens to the Cry of the Poor Man, his Cloud
Over London in volume terrific, low bended in anger.

Rintrah & Palamabron view the Human Harvest beneath.
Their Wine-presses & Barns stand open; the Ovens are prepar'd;
The Waggons ready; terrific Lions & Tygers sport & play.
All Animals upon the Earth are prepar'd in all their strength

[PLATE 45]
To go forth to the Great Harvest & Vintage of the Nations.

Finis

PART THREE

COMMENTARY

To read William Blake's illuminated books is to participate in a spiritual education. To read Blake's *Milton* is to discover the nature of that spiritual education concurrent with the education itself. Consequently, Blake's *Milton* does not exist solely as an object of admiration or study. Although *Milton* is incredibly beautiful in its combination of word and illustration and although its complexity stimulates intellectual scrutiny, it is a prophecy and, like all prophecy, it provides spiritual instruction. William Blake is a spiritual teacher, a prophet who, having "discover'd the infinite in every thing" is committed to "raising other men into a perception of the infinite" (*The Marriage of Heaven and Hell*). And, *Milton* is the book in which Blake teaches how "all the Lord's people" can become prophets. In *Milton* Blake defines the spiritual journey which renews prophecy in every moment of human time.

THE JOURNEY

Milton is an autobiographical poem in which Blake charts the processes of his own prophetic education. However, *Milton* is not a traditional autobiography with Blake as its main character. Blake designates John Milton, the seventeenth-century Christian poet, to be the central figure of *Milton* and, in this way, acknowledges that John Milton was his literary and spiritual teacher. As Milton undertakes a spiritual journey within Blake's narrative, it is as if John Milton and his works are teaching Blake about their identity and simultaneously guiding Blake to discovery of his poetic and prophetic role. Therefore, only at the conclusion of *Milton* does Blake achieve the infinite vision which enables him to be the prophet narrator of *Milton*. And, only at the conclusion of the poem does Blake's reader understand the processes which have encouraged the composition of *Milton*. Blake's reader, then, undertakes a spiritual journey through *Milton*, as does William Blake. Both Blake and his reader are led to that journey by Blake's character John Milton who, through his own journey, witnesses in *Milton* to the meaning and effectiveness of the spiritual path.

Initiating a spiritual journey requires realization of error and the loving acceptance of the journey and of the teacher. After hearing the Bard, who represents the ancient authority of Poetic Genius, the purveyor of ancient and eternal truths, Milton rises from "the heavens of Albion ardorous," to undertake his pilgrimage. The Bard's song is a vision of how Milton erred in justifying the ways of God to men. Milton accepts the Bard's teaching that his reasoning power, his Spectre, his Selfhood, has been the source of his error. But, not only does Milton passively accept, he actively claims his error: "I in my Selfhood am that Satan; I am that Evil One!" Milton realizes that just as Satan was an agent of fragmentation in the Bard's song, Milton himself had strengthened the fragmentation of existence in his works. In *Paradise Lost*, especially, he had created a Natural Religion which divided God from Satan, heaven from hell, the divine from the human. Consequently, Milton, experiencing the Bard's song in eternity, realizes the error of his mortal vision as it abides on earth in his works, his sixfold emanation. He knows he must confront and transform the error in his work in order to resolve the disparity between his eternal and mortal perspectives. Then, as the Bard takes "refuge in Milton's bosom," Milton becomes one with his teacher. Milton's spiritual journey thus demonstrates the Bard's wisdom; Milton will constitute, embody, the words of salvation the Bard provides.

Spiritual travel includes confrontation with error, a testing process. Throughout his journey Milton confronts projections of his selfhood, images of his error, obstacles to the pilgrim's spiritual growth. Among these obstacles, he beholds his own shadow on the verge of Beulah, the hermaphroditic reflection of his error, but despite its "mournful form double," he enters into it. Later, he is opposed by Los who, "in fibrous strength," shooting his limbs "forth like roots of trees against the forward path / Of Milton's journey," represents the "fibrous strength" of Milton's own poetry, a poetry of Natural Religion. Los also represents Milton's false prophecy, his natural rather than spiritual truth. Nevertheless, Milton labors "with his journey" until he meets Urizen, "the Demon cold," who baptizes Milton with the "icy fluid" of rational power, but Milton counters the baptism by sculpting Urizen a new body, thus "giving a body to Falsehood that it may be cast off forever" (*Jerusalem*). In Blake's illustration of this scene (plate 15), Urizen appears as Moses carrying the Tablets of the Law, as the false priest of Milton's Natural Religion. Additionally, Milton is lured by Rahab and Tirzah and "all their sons & daughters," a second "Twofold form Hermaphroditic." They offer Milton an earthly Kingship through the power of Natural Religion, the monarchical model of religion Milton erected in *Paradise Lost*. This, too, Milton declines. Ultimately Milton faces the virgin, Ololon, and Satan himself. Ololon, although mild—hence a twelve-year-old virgin—distinctly calls upon Milton's restrained desire, that hypocritical Puritan morality which exalts virginity and equates the body with

136

sin. Satan, who embodies all Milton's error, entices Milton to use his own power, a power Milton knows he possesses, to annihilate Satan. Milton, in refusing Satan, uses wisdom to overcome the most difficult test of his journey. Satan, the state of error, cannot be destroyed but must be "new Created continually," so that each individual will have a state or context in which to place his own error that it might be "annihilated alway." The laws of Satan's "false Heav'ns" decree a power struggle with a continuous cycle of greater replacing greater. Milton knows that in annihilating his own error, his Satanic selfhood, he does not and can not annihilate Satan for others: a spiritual journey is always individual. No one person should pretend to offer corporate salvation; "each shall mutually / Annihilate himself for others' good." Each traveler may serve as exemplar, as teacher, but the teacher does not master the student. Such emphasis on mastery would decree the perpetuation of hypocrisy and self-righteousness, those wonders of Satan's holiness Milton surpasses.

When Milton refuses to annihilate Satan, he achieves the transformation of the spiritual journey. He has recognized his eternal identity, and he understands completely his Satanic selfhood, the adversary to Milton's infinite vision. Milton has exposed his error and revealed his divine vision through the spiritual journey. Thus, Milton affirms the truth of prophecy and the role of the prophet. In his prophetic works, the prophet exposes error continually that each individual may annihilate error within himself. Thereby, the prophet shows each individual how he may perceive the infinite in everything.

Since the traveler must stand open and naked, Milton sheds the "robe of the promise" and ungirds himself "from the oath of God" at the beginning of his journey (magnificently represented by the title-page illustration and plate 16). Because it requires complete honesty and openness, the journey is painful. Spiritual travel demands sacrifice of all the traveler thinks he is: his old identity, his ego, his comfortable and secure points of reference. Then, in surrendering all he has assumed himself to be, the traveler survives without identity, feeling weak and empty, in uncertainty and chaos, like Milton "a wanderer lost in dreary night." Milton has no anticipation of gain to replace his loss; if he has, he has failed the most important test of the journey. Significantly, Milton enters "self annihilation and eternal death" questioning "When will the Resurrection come?" The spiritual path, Milton senses, requires giving, not getting. Sacrifice and surrender and giving mean a painful renunciation, but they also can be an equally painful openness to love. Milton, in response to his teacher, the Bard, rises up "ardorous," loving. Just as the journey is undertaken because of love, so too the relationship upon which the journey is predicated, the relationship between student and teacher, must be loving and mutual, "each shall mutually / Annihilate himself." The Bard loves and therefore sings. His song does not cater to Milton's "present ease or gratification" (*The Marriage of Heaven and Hell*); it, in fact, opposes Milton. But Milton accepts the opposition in the loving spirit in which it is offered. Blake believes that "Opposition is true Friendship" (*The Marriage of Heaven and Hell*). He sees the teacher/student relationship as neither "corporeal" nor hierarchical, but as a loving and mutual conversation: the Bard takes "refuge in Milton's bosom."

Like Milton in Blake's poem, the loving reader of Blake journeys into recognition of his selfhood, that error in perception which limits imaginative and spiritual growth. Reading *Milton* is thus a journey of unlearning. Blake describes his task in *Milton* as displaying "Nature's cruel holiness, the deceits of Natural Religion." In other words, one of the basic tasks of Blake's poem is to expose the false reality of the so-called "natural world" and its assertion that it is the only reality. This false reality is a result of the selfhood of each reader; it is that world we naturally perceive as "without," the world we externalize and desire to control and which in turn controls us. Consequently, Blake's vision of the world is so dissonant with our usual understanding that we must "unlearn"; we must give up our preconceptions about the world and about ourselves within that world.

Some of us are surprised to learn that the world beyond the body is uncertain, yet one of the basic tenets of Einstein and scientific methods after him is the impossibility of separating the observer from his observations. That is to say, our perception of events beyond the body is the result of our views about the nature of reality. Blake thought that we become what we behold. For this reason, he sets out to transform the relationships between the perceiver and perceived by guiding his reader into a journey of spiritual discovery. It is important that we perceive not from the selfhood, that aggregate of biases, prejudices, and hypocrisies which in its dogmatic desire for control negates our potential and becomes our existence, but that we perceive within an attitude of surrender, thereby opening to worlds of eternity. Modern psychologists have catalogued at length the assumptions of orthodox Western psychology, the assumptions that often form the nature of the modern reader's selfhood and its perceptions. The chief of these may be summarized as follows: a person is his body and nothing more; each person is isolated from all others, locked in his nervous system; consciousness is identical with the activity of the brain; death is the termination of human consciousness; a person perceives the physical world and obtains sensations from the internal operations of his body and nervous system; a person can trust his senses to inform him accurately about the nature of the physical world. It is crucial to reading *Milton* for us to understand that these assumptions of the modern world view were developed as a direct result of the scientific revolution of Blake's time, and that they are the assumptions underlying what may be called a worship of the physical world or what Blake, in fact, called Natural Religion. For the men of science, who are heirs to the discoveries of Bacon, Newton, and Locke, there is only the physical world. Like many pagan religions which sought to know their god in order that they could learn to control him with worship and sacrifices, so too, the priests of Natural Religion seek to understand the physical world in all its intricacies so it might be conquered or at least controlled. Those of us educated in this scientific world view—who earn our livings through the advanced technologies developed from it, and enjoy comfort as a result of its radical transformations of daily life—constantly dwell in an environment fabricated out of these assumptions. Our laws, our institutions, our understandings of sanity and insanity, and many of our basic cultural codes and social conventions imply the "truths" of this Natural Religion.

According to Blake, the individual living by such "truths" equates his identity with his physical body; he trusts his senses to inform him accurately about the objective world and is, thus, "shut in narrow doleful form." Such people are isolated: "folded within themselves," they see only the "Vegetable Ratio" and deny the eternal perspectives of the spirit. Blake would say that because we have hardened our optic nerves into opaque bones, we perceive the world without as a "black pebble." This reciprocity of perception is a "dull round" (*There is No Natural Religion*, First Series); it is death, the termination of what Blake would have called consciousness, the human and, therefore, eternal perception. Instead, Blake urges a person to see himself "like the diamond which, tho' cloth'd / In rugged covering in the mine, is open all within, / And in his hallow'd center holds the heavens of bright eternity." This reciprocity of perception is imagination, the world of body and spirit, the world where "God is within & without" (*Jerusalem*).

Therefore, although it might be natural for us to expect an author to base his world upon a scientific view of the human condition and for us to read according to our scientific heritage, to do so, would be to insist that Blake's work conform to the boundaries of our perception. We thereby would confine Blake's work within our expectations of what a poem should be: linear and rational, with an obvious clarity, and a cause-effect structure. Instead the reader must enter *Milton* loving Blake, letting Blake take refuge in the reader. Milton's reaction to the Bard's song, his epiphany of recognition, exemplifies the kind of reaction Blake seeks from his reader; it is that transforming vision which launches the pilgrim upon his quest for spiritual knowledge; without it no journey, no quest, is possible. If we fail to enter *Milton* lovingly we could become judgmental; we could attempt to assert control over Blake's text. Then we would be the tyrant readers Blake would deplore. If the reader surrenders to Blake and opens to Blake's teaching, however, then *Milton* manifests potential for the reader's regeneration. The reader's task, consequently, is to acknowledge the relationship between the reality he has grown accustomed to thinking of as "normal waking consciousness" and the prophetic, visionary universe Blake creates within *Milton*. The crucial difference between *Milton* and most poetic fiction is that Blake is making a serious proposal for a visionary reality contrary to the scientific vision which comes naturally to us. Blake asks us to see *Milton* not as fiction but as truth. Like Milton's journey, the journey of reading *Milton* will not be easy. Blake tests our patience and endurance at every turn—with complex patterns of allusion, with disorientations of time and space, with assaults on our demands for logic and consistency in spelling, punctuation, and grammar. Yet, there is wealth and richness in opening and surrendering to *Milton*, since within *Milton* is exemplified the journey towards that moment which "renovates every Moment of the Day," the expansion of imagination through prophetic truth.

THE GEOGRAPHY OF THE JOURNEY

Blake constructs an elaborate geography for the prophetic education *Milton* contains. The settings range from the biographical, Blake's Lambeth and Felpham residences, to the eternal England and the Biblical Palestine, to the places of Blake's mythology. But Blake demonstrates consistently in his works that all settings are created by perception. Despite *Milton's* many settings, therefore, there is only one geography for Blake from which all settings are derived—the human body and its anatomy and physiology of perception. And, Blake believed that the human body is the flesh and blood of divinity. Because "God becomes as we are, that we may be as he is" (*There is No Natural Religion*, Second Series), Blake thought that we inhabit a human form divine which incarnates the Human Form Divine of Jesus. When an individual perceives his divine body, he will open to eternal, visionary perspectives.

This geography is based upon Blake's rejection of two basic rationalistic premises: 1) that sensory data are the sole determinants in ascertaining the nature of the physical world and 2) that only the physical world exists. These assumptions derive from the physical sciences' rejection of the soul as the focus for participation in this world and a concomitant rejection of the soul's eternal, infinite, and immortal point of awareness. For Blake the physical body's sensory organs, separated from the soul's imaginative powers, are limited and flawed. If, as Blake assumes, at its center the universe has an eternal, infinite, and immortal reality, then how can a limited, finite, and mortal observer who refuses to acknowledge that center, know the state of true existence? When an individual's sensory organs are "folded within themselves," how can he behold the "great light"? Using the eye as representative of all organs of sensation, and sight as the emblem of all sensation, Blake admonishes us to see *through* the eye, not *with* the eye (*The Everlasting Gospel*): to see as if "Body is a portion of Soul discern'd by the five Senses" (*The Marriage of Heaven and Hell*), not with the body exclusively, as if it were separate from the soul. In other words, we must see with the soul observing reality as if it were the body, since the body by itself alone sees a lie, the human delusion. Blake clearly seems to have thought that sensation or feeling proceeds inward from the sense organs to the functioning brain, where the sensory information is received and interpreted by the agency of the soul in conjunction with the vegetable memory. Once this sensory information is received by the vegetable memory, which contains the individual's learned experience, including the assumptions he has been taught to make about the world, an interpretive reality is projected outward upon the world according to the individual's powers of perception. "As a man is, So he Sees," says Blake (Letter to Dr. Trusler, 23 August 1799). If the senses perceive only the literal "Vegetable Ratio," then there is nothing beyond the brain but a sensory tumult, a horrible chaos in which nothing is permanent and nothing lasts. Paradoxically, this chaos *seems* rational and orderly, but as Blake says, this is a "delusion of Ulro." According to such a viewpoint, the individual who "sees the Ratio only, sees himself only"; he projects his rational selfhood onto the physical world. But if an individual sees with the soul, his senses discover "the Infinite in all things" (*There is No Natural Religion*, Second Series) and the wondrous regions of eternity.

Blake complicates our attempts to understand his vision of physical reality by his assertion that the earth is concave and not convex. We find it very difficult to visualize the concave geography in the world within *Milton*, because our culture has insisted on the opposite curvature. Nonetheless, if we are to successfully comprehend the visionary landscape inherent in the poem, and upon which the characters move, we must continually remind ourselves that we are working with concavities, caverns and chasms, rather than with our familiar convexities, rounded slopes and mountains. Blake describes the earth as concave, as a cavern of "labyrinthine intricacy"; this earth is the human skull or body which, if observed from without, is convex but, if observed from within, is concave. Similarly Blake describes the sky as an "immortal Tent"; man "standing on his own roof, or in his garden" sees such concave space as his universe; he sees from within to without. Because this is true, Blake insists that the astronomer's model of the earth as "a Globe rolling thro' Voidness" is a delusion, for such would be the model of an earth separated from its perceiver. In a concave model, however, all the earth, the sky, the universe are within man's immediate perception.

This view of the physical world attests that Blake has returned the physical body of the individual, and the soul within it, to the center of his cosmos as the medieval world view had done before him. This is the Vitruvian man, the man in the center of a circle proscribed by the extensions of his limbs. Here, however, Blake's universe is proscribed not by a conceptual framework of geography and terrain, but only by the sensory horizon, the limits of an individual's perception. Stand a man in his garden, or in a tower, and his universe is literally, Blake would say, everything he sees. In a world view based upon the notion that we create the vision of the external world by our own projections, this is necessarily the case. What Blake asserts, then, is that it is our interaction with perceived objects which is the essential element of reality.

Just as the Vitruvian man stands in the center of his circle, we stand in a perceptual concavity which is much like a great sensory balloon. Blake calls this concavity the Mundane Egg. This concave egg may be seen from reasoning perception—the perception that only the body and its senses exist—as a limiting and imprisoning reality. From the viewpoint of the reasoning mind the labyrinthine concave egg constitutes our reality; its concave shell becomes a sensory horizon. It and all within it constitute the "Limit of Opacity" beyond which our senses do not penetrate. Within the shell or circumference we see, then, a surging chaos, a sensory tumult with which our sensory organs must interact to select and interpret data. Blake names the chaos Ulro. In attempting to understand and make sense of this chaos we proscribe a limiting surface upon it, a limiting surface which reinforces the shell as the outermost limit of opacity. In other words, we make the shell more opaque. To this limiting concave surface, which is comparable to the concave membrane lining the inner surface of the egg, Blake gives the name Entuthon Benython. (Ulro, then, like the shell itself, surrounds and underlies Entuthon Benython.) He pictures Entuthon Benython as impenetrable forests and "deeps." It is all the opaque surfaces we think we see, all the opaque surfaces a reasoning mind erects in its attempt to know and hence control the universe: the surface of perceived objects, the surface of the body, the surfaces of the earth and the apparent surface of the sky. All the space between the surfaces we think we see beyond and the surface of our body, the empty space we feel we must control, Blake names Udan-Adan, and he defines Udan-Adan as "a Lake not of Waters but of Spaces" (*The Four Zoas*). Udan-Adan is enclosed by Entuthon Benython, and both are enclosed within Ulro. Seen as a convex surface, Entuthon Benython becomes a world with an empty core (Udan-Adan), hanging suspended within chaos (Ulro), much as John Milton's "pendant world," in *Paradise Lost*, created by what Blake considered a god of reason, hangs suspended within chaos, fastened by a golden chain to heaven. Ulro, Entuthon Benython, and Udan-Adan are the spaces created by a Satanic selfhood and its limiting perception. They are the spaces of error, the regions into which Milton travels to annihilate his selfhood in Blake's poem.

Ulro, Entuthon Benython, and Udan-Adan are the spaces the Bard identifies as created by Enitharmon to receive the falling Satan; as such, they are spaces of mercy—spaces which exist so that they may be annihilated continually, spaces within which a spiritual journey is possible. Blake believes that as a consequence of vision from within, the result of the spiritual journey, the spaces of the "dull round" (Entuthon Benython, Udan-Adan, and Ulro) are transformed into energizing, formative spaces, wherein all the component parts of the body and its universe may be formed into human lineaments, the contours of an eternal body. Within these transformed spaces, form and beauty are created "around the dark regions of sorrow, / Giving to airy nothing a name and a habitation / Delightful: with bounds to the Infinite putting off the Indefinite / Into most holy forms of Thought." Blake calls these spaces Allamanda, Bowlahoola, and Golgonooza.

Allamanda is that region of intellection called Commerce, the "Cultivated Land / Around the City of Golgonooza." Here the plowing and harrowing of the Bard's song go on. Clearly, within the body, Allamanda is the functioning synergy of the nervous system. The plowing image may refer to the "furrows" of the brain and connotes mental cultivation. Cultivation entails not only preparation of the soil for planting by plowing it up and by harrowing the large clods of earth into finer, looser soil, but also the plowing under of crops as green fertilizer to enrich the soil—a process emblematic of the plowing under of preconceptions, opaque surfaces, to make way for growth. Mental cultivation refers to enrichment of the mind by learning, training, and participating in the spiritual journey. This is why, in *Milton*, we hear so much of plowing and replowing, with harvest always to come. Consequently, a lifetime, as Blake views it, should be spent in continual cultivation and harvest. Allamanda involves communication, learning, and the exchange of ideas—the continual activities of mental harvest. Its counterpart is Bowlahoola, "the Stomach in every individual." As Allamanda is the nervous system, Bowlahoola is the system of organs within the body which support the nervous system. And, as Allamanda is the plowed ground, Bowlahoola is like the sun and energy which warm it. In addition, Allamanda produces the bread of the eternal body in its harvest, and Bowlahoola produces the energizing blood of the body in its wine-press. Yet Bowlahoola is more, for it includes the heart and lungs, the same set of organs in which Los's forge, bellows, and hammer are located. We are told by Blake that in Bowlahoola "the various Classes of Men are all mark'd out determinate," because different men have different energy levels, not according to the natural spaces of Udan-Adan but "by Spiritual power alone." Bowlahoola is called Law because, in the body, its activities mirror the functions societies ask of law, the regulation of space and production of human energy. Finally, Golgonooza which includes both Allamanda and Bowlahoola "is nam'd Art & Manufacture." Golgonooza is a country and a city within that country. In this way Blake's portrait of Golgonooza resembles a medieval city-state. The state surrounds the city, supplying material for the sustenance of the city. Thus Allamanda and Bowlahoola represent the country which supplies sustenance to the city of Golgonooza.

Golgonooza, the "Universe" of Los and Enitharmon "is built eternally" to show an individual how to transform the spaces of Ulro. Los and Enitharmon act in love and mercy toward fallen humanity; they represent attributes of the artist; they appropriately reside in Golgonooza, the city and nation of art. Los is called Time, and we learn in *Milton* that his hammers are the beating heart, the bellows of his forge are the lungs, and his furnaces are the stomach. For Blake, then, time is a function of pulsation, the rhythmic pounding of the heart, the rhythmic surge of air in the lungs, and the rhythm of digestion in the stomach and intestines. The sensation of the passage of time is inherent in the pulse which pervades the tissues of the body. Los, as the poet/prophet who perceives the rhythms in life, witnesses to the truth that "Time is the mercy of Eternity; without Time's swiftness / Which is the swiftest of all things, all were eternal torment." Enitharmon is called Space; her implements are the looms. She is a weaver who creates the web of the body which is the web of death and also, mercifully, the web of life, for without life there can be no death or release of the spirit to eternal perspectives. Enitharmon and her daughters, then, have as their charge the creation of lovely spaces from the fibers of life; the beauty of the natural world, the beauty of the physical body, the beauty of a work of art, are the result of Enitharmon's care.

Because Blake believed that "whatever can be Created can be Annihilated," he considered the spaces of Ulro, Entuthon Benython, and Udan-Adan, as well as Golgonooza, Allamanda, and Bowlahoola, to be created settings. An individual can create or perceive a fallacious, illusory world as easily as he can create or perceive a productive world. Moreover, it is possible to fall out of a productive world into illusion. Consequently, Blake asserts that visionary perspective must be new created every moment of the day. In order to affirm the existence of eternal life and eternal perspectives, Blake sees that these spaces possess archetypal and eternal parallels which can never be annihilated. They underlie all perception. Thus, Blake allows for change and growth in life, but he also affirms that change and growth have eternal, archetypal direction. Blake calls these archetypal regions Eden, Beulah, and Golgonooza. Eden, Blake saw as a beautiful garden in whose beams of light "the Human Harvest waves abundant" (*Jerusalem*). Eden is the archetypal form of the Garden and the Harvest. It represents the eternal potential for transformation of the forest of Entuthon Benython into the harvested ground of Allamanda. Beulah, Blake perceived as a "pleasant lovely Shadow," a place of "mild & pleasant Rest," where "Contrarieties are equally True." Beulah, like Bowlahoola, is an energizing space, but it, unlike Bowlahoola, energizes through rest not through vigorous activity. Thereby Blake conveys with Beulah the archetype for revitalization. Appropriately, Beulah is, in Blake's geography, the place where the poetic muses reside, and the muses by their powers of inspiration continually revitalize the state of poetry by inspiring new poems. Moreover, just as poetry and all artistic activities fill the emptiness of life with words, designs, and music so, too, Beulah is the archetype which promises that art will exist eternally as a counter to the lake of empty spaces Udan-Adan represents. Golgonooza is the only space that Blake considered to be both a created space and an eternal archetypal form. As a created space Golgonooza is any work of art—a book, a poem, a painting. As an archetype Golgonooza is the eternal pattern for all such creations. As city and country of art, then, it represents the active imagination creating individual eternal identity through works of art, and it represents the imagination —the prophetic, visionary perception, which is the "Human Existence" itself. Since "travellers to Eternity pass inward to Golgonooza," Golgonooza becomes a passageway to eternity as well as the eternal reminder that such journeys are ever potential for the artist and his audience through a work of art.

Thus, we see nine regions in Blake's geography: the eternal spaces of Eden, Beulah, and Golgonooza; the created spaces of Allamanda, Bowlahoola, and Golgonooza; and the illusory spaces of Entuthon Benython, Udan-Adan, and Ulro.

We propose that the nine regions of the geography may be further understood through a conflation of Blake's map on plate 32 of *Milton* with the sup-

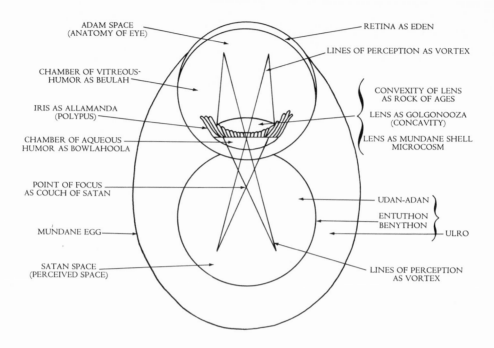

FIGURE 1. A Proposed Model for the Visionary Geography of *Milton*

posed workings of the sensorium and the anatomy of the eye. Within the spaces of this map on plate 32, may be seen the residence of the soul within the brain case and the anatomy of the eye as emblem of perception (Figure 1). Blake, it should be recalled, believed this to be a visionary world, a world created by perception from within. It was therefore a world with the soul as focus of perception. The scientists of Blake's day knew very little about the function of the living brain, and, consequently, they employed the term "sensorium" in reference to the living brain, as opposed to the dead brain known from dissection. The sensorium, then, was the space to which all sensation was brought and from which all perception proceeded, determined, it was supposed, by the action of an observer-soul. Blake, it would seem, discovered in the anatomy of the eye and in an understanding of its optics a precise image of the processes of his visionary soul-centered world. Blake was a man with both a comprehensive graphic imagination and skill in the graphic arts developed from his training as a commercial engraver. Since it appears that Blake carefully mapped his spaces in *Milton* with a graphic artist's attention to minute detail and precise interrelationships, a discussion of this visionary anatomy will assist in opening

Milton's spaces for the modern reader. Our definitions of the anatomy and physiology of the eye are drawn from the *Rees Cyclopaedia*, a work published from 1802 until 1820 for which Blake did seven engravings; thereby we suggest this is knowledge about the eye potentially available to Blake (Figure 2).

The map on plate 32 is Blake's map of consciousness, and the spaces he charts within it contain much of his understanding of the eternal nature of human experience. There are three major elements of this map: four external globes, a central egg-shaped space, and two internal spaces designated "Adam" and "Satan." The four globes labeled Urizen, Tharmas, Urthona, and Luvah represent the origins of consciousness, the Four Zoas who stood around the throne of the Eternal Man, Albion, before his fall. Albion is "our Ancestor, patriarch of the Atlantic Continent, whose History Preceded that of the Hebrews & in whose Sleep, or Chaos, Creation began" (*A Vision of the Last Judgment*). Albion is the archetypal man, the pattern of all consciousness. The Four Zoas are the four eternal and archetypal faculties of Man. Urthona is the Imagination; Luvah is Passion; Urizen is Reason; and Tharmas is Instinct. The cause of the present state of things, Blake says in his myth of Albion's fall, is Albion's envy of the Divine Vision, that is to say, Albion's refusal to surrender his separate identity in the recognition that he and Jesus were one man, "mutual in love

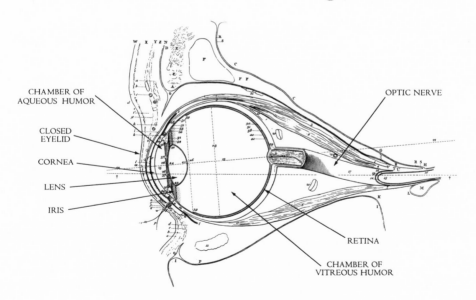

CHAMBER OF
AQUEOUS HUMOR

CLOSED
EYELID

CORNEA

LENS

IRIS

OPTIC NERVE

RETINA

CHAMBER OF
VITREOUS HUMOR

FIGURE 2. Enlarged Diagram of the Eye

147

Urthona = Imag. & Los is an aspect of Urthona

divine" (*Jerusalem*). When Albion fell, the Four Zoas "fell towards the Center in dire ruin, sinking down" forming the Universe of Los. Los himself is an aspect of Urthona. He is the eternal prophet who guards the divine vision in time of trouble. Los's task is to guard the organs of perception so that renovation of this ruined existence is possible. Thus these four globes surrounding the "Egg form'd World of Los" represent "a dark land of death, of fiery corroding waters, / Where lie in evil death the Four Immortals pale and cold." The central egg-shaped space is the macrocosmic universe of Los in which the prophet/bard ceaselessly pursues his Mental Fight to return human consciousness to the perception of the infinite. This is the Mundane Egg which contains the sensorium, the residence of the soul of each individual. Blake realized that all reality was within the human brain, that the sensory organs sent all sensory data to the living brain where reality was fabricated. Thus to the individual whose "mortal brain is wall'd and moated round / Within," this space contains only the sensory tumult of Ulro. From this perspective the Mundane Egg seems to be Ulro. Then the illusory Satan world is the only reality produced, because the human body sees itself only. The opaque surfaces of the phenomenal world enclose all reality as the lining of the egg seems to enclose all the contents of the egg. However, as we begin our spiritual journey following Milton's path into the perception of the infinite in all things, we begin to understand that this egg is also the human body, which "in its inward form / Is a garden of delight & a building of magnificence, / Built by the Sons of Los in Bowlahoola & Allamanda." Finally, we may understand this egg to contain all the universe of conscious experience of the individual and the spiritual existence of "a brain open to heaven & hell, / Withinside wondrous & expansive, its gates are not clos'd." The Satan space (Ulro, Entuthon Benython, and Udan-Adan) is the world "seen in fallacy outside" when bodily sensations dominate perception: it is the Ulro delusion, the world of Natural Religion. It is, therefore, properly diagrammed outside the eye. However, when the Satan space is seen from within, viewed by the soul within the sensorium shell, it is renovated into the Adam space (Golgonooza, Allamanda, and Bowlahoola)—a visionary space with analogues in the body. It may be seen that the Adam space has analogues within the anatomy and physiology of the eye, because Blake uses the eye to represent all activity within the body. Thereby, illusion becomes imaginative reality.

Within Blake's map on plate 32, we can now see the hidden geography of the Adam and Satan spaces. To stress the redemption of vision, Blake, in the Adam space, inverts the three-dimensional relationships of the Satan world, where, within chaos, a lake of spaces is defined by a forest. The city of Golgonooza centers the Adam space; it is surrounded in a three-dimensional view by Alla-

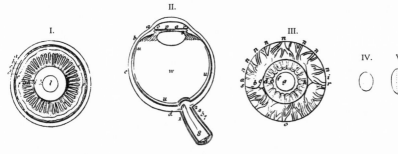

I. CROSS-SECTION OF EYE LOOKING DOWN ON LENS AND IRIS FROM RETINA

II. LONGITUDINAL CROSS-SECTION OF EYE

III. HORIZONTAL CROSS-SECTION OF EYE IRIS WITHOUT LENS

IV., V., VI. EXAMPLES OF LENS

FIGURE 3. Anatomy of Eye—Descriptions of Golgonooza

manda, beneath which Bowlahoola is situated (Figure 3). Thus, Blake pictures not a world suspended within a void, but a world centered in creativity. Since Blake describes Golgonooza as having "Domes," he has located it within the crystalline domes of the multi-layered lens of the eye. The lens, while small, is an egg-shaped world unto itself within the eye, a microcosm of the Mundane Egg; it is a microcosm of vision, since it brings all the light rays impinging upon the eye into focus and sends forth rays as the lines of perception. Similarly, Golgonooza is the microcosm for Blake's world of art, bringing perception into focus through art and sending forth visionary communication as does a work of art. Further, we can see that the light rays impinging on the lens and the rays of perception emanating from it correspond to the "intellectual spears, & long winged arrows of thought" (*Jerusalem*) which are Blake's emblems for the mutual interchange between art and its audience, that mutual interchange for which Golgonooza is the setting. And, with the Mundane Egg surrounding the Satan and Adam spaces mirrored in the mundane egg of the lens, rebirth is firmly established as the necessary activity of art.

Since Allamanda is the plowed ground around the city of Golgonooza, Blake has placed it within the iris which, in the eye, surrounds the lens. Consequently, Bowlahoola, which Blake indicates as being beneath Allamanda, would be parallel to the cornea and its chamber of aqueous humor in the eye. These seem appropriate relationships, especially when the aqueous humor, which disperses and amplifies light rays proceeding into the eye, is compared to Bowlahoola, where Blake places the heart, lungs and stomach—organs which disperse, distribute, and amplify energy within the human body; or when the iris, which causes the pupil to dilate and contract, thus influencing the amount of light let into the eye, is compared to Allamanda where plowing and harrowing, the mental cultivation, open the visionary eye to eternity. The country and city of Golgonooza, then, are the locations of harvest and of vintage. Golgonooza is a place of energy and cultivation. Therefore, Golgonooza is the setting where artistic form is given to the human body, and Golgonooza with its formative powers redeems mortality to eternity.

It is especially valuable to see the eternal forms (Beulah, Eden, and Golgonooza) as existing within Blake's understanding of the anatomy and physiology of perception. Blake saw Beulah in terms which parallel a description of the chamber of vitreous humor within the eye. Beulah as a passageway for travelers to and from eternity parallels the vitreous humor which is a passageway for the rays of light as they converge into foci upon the retina. Moreover, just as the vitreous humor functions to keep the surface of the retina uniformly spherical, so Beulah functions to protect and preserve "love & pity & sweet compassion." Eden, Blake describes as if it were the retina of the eye. Eden's harvest/garden descriptions are analogous to the retina's reticulated surface. Eden opens into eternity just as the retina is connected to the optic nerve. The impression of light rays upon the retina produces perception, just as Eden's eternal beams shine outward to Golgonooza, opening that center and expanding the ever-enduring doors of art and the creative individual. Eden transmits the images it receives to Golgonooza where they take form. Since light rays impressing upon the retina produce inverted images, Eden mirrors the Ulro world and redeems its eternal potential through Golgonooza and art.

In order to understand Blake's vision of perception, the mutual nature of the perceptual process must be stressed. Perception both flows inward to the eye as a stream of sensory data entering the brain, and outward from the eye, as a projection of reality upon the sensory tumult beyond the body. Blake, having merged with the Bard, Milton, and Los, becomes the prophetic narrator of *Milton*, uniquely able to describe both the outer (finite) and inner (infinite) sides of perception and Milton's journey. Consequently, we may understand that Milton's path through the terrain of the anatomy of perception (a descent which is different from Milton's track into Blake's consciousness as indicated on plate 32) reverses the flow of light, which as it is reflected from an object, passes through the cornea, iris, lens, and chamber of vitreous humor before the light rays land upon the retina. Milton, thus, rises up from the Heavens of Albion/Eden/retina, journeys through the shadowy realm of Beulah and encounters the corpse of Albion upon the Rock of Ages. The Rock of Ages is the lens seen as a convex surface, while the lens is Golgonooza seen as a concave surface. The lens neatly replicates the Rock of Ages, since the fingers of the iris seem to embrace the lens as if it were a rock "inwrapped with the weeds of death." Moreover, since the lens is near the surface of the body, it is fair to describe it as if it were a rock around which the sea of time and space thunders. Milton falls through the lens and cornea, through Udan-Adan, and into Blake's foot.

For his description of perception, Blake employs five major images, all of which specify the characteristics of a spiritual journey: the vortex, the polypus, the couch of death, the lark, and Golgonooza. And, like the perceptual process, a spiritual journey can proceed from eternity as Milton travels, or to eternity as Blake travels; both journeys can converge in a work of art such as Blake's *Milton*.

Blake's image of spiritual travel is the vortex. Since Blake insists that "every thing has its / Own Vortex," his poetry and designs abound with a variety of figures which invoke the vortex. The essential image beneath all these figures is the tunnel, and given the position from which the tunnel is seen, it may seem to assume all these parallel figures. When the observer is standing within the vortex looking directly upon its whirling center, it assumes a circular appearance as if it were a broad disk. If, as in the designs of plate 16 and plate 21, the vortical disk originates in eternity, then it seems to be a sun, and here in these designs Milton and Los are rising up out of eternity to enter the sea of time and space. When the vortex is delivering the traveler into the chaos, then it is dark, and we may see only a whirling cloud, as Milton does on the title-page design. If the observer is standing slightly to the side of the vortex so that only an arc of the bright inner surface is seen with its center obscured by the dark rim of the tunnel, then the vortex as the new or old moon is seen. If the vortex is dark, and light is seen through it only in points, then it assumes the characteristics of a constellation or a starry universe. If the observer is outside the vortex and observing its passage, it may look like a comet, its fiery tail indicating the path of the traveler. If the vortex contains a man, it may take the appearance of a five-pointed star, one point marking each of the man's appendages. Thus, on plate 2 the star-vortex marks Milton's entrance into the vortex as he rises up "ardorous." The stars on plates 14, 29, and 33 all trail behind them similar wedges of streaming light, marking the cone of the vortex through which Milton travels. Even the flower seems to be a vortex, as its shape mirrors the cone of a vortex.

Blake knew that spiritual travel actually opens the traveler to infinity, redeeming the limits of opacity and contraction the reasoning mind imposes upon existence. For Blake "there is no Limit of Expansion; there is no Limit of Translucence / In the bosom of Man for ever from eternity to eternity" (*Jerusalem*). But if everything has its own vortex, then the thin membrane of opacity which closes off our world from eternity is an illusion, and we are open within and without to limitless translucence. Blake clarifies the nature of the vortex in *Jerusalem*—

> The Vegetative Universe opens like a flower from the Earth's Center
> In which is Eternity. It expands in Stars to the Mundane Shell
> And there it meets Eternity again, both within and without.

The flower as vortex also appears in *Milton*, where the flowers in their "innumerable Dance" send "forth their precious Odours" and from their small centers "Eternity expands." Thus, as the vortex expands from eternity within the earth's center or within a flower's center, it expands as well from the stars to the earth; the vortex is "both within and without"; the earth is "one infinite plane," if we see our journey upon it as a dynamic vortex.

If the vortex is not perceived by the traveler, if he is not open to the "infinite plane," the vortex becomes the polypus, Blake's image for enclosure within the vegetable world. The polypus is a term for a "bisexual, aquatic insect," the hydra, and for the devouring sea anemone whose oscillating tentacles draw small fish into its body cavity. It is also a surgical term for a diseased and often cancerous growth, which affixes itself to the internal surfaces of the body; this growth, always destructive, is especially horrible if it attacks the uterus. Blake describes it in *Jerusalem* as "a ravening eating Cancer growing in the Female, / A Polypus of Roots, of Reasoning, Doubt, Despair & Death." And, in *Milton* Los warns Palamabron and Rintrah about such a uterine polypus and advises them to give all their "strength against Eternal Death" lest they all become vegetated. Los continues: "were it not for Bowlahoola & Allamanda / No Human Form, but only a Fibrous Vegetation, / A Polypus of soft affections without Thought or Vision / Must tremble in the Heavens & Earths thro' all the Ulro space." Los cautions that if Allamanda and Bowlahoola are negated during the process of weaving a vegetable body over the mortal soul gestating, the result is, not a living infant, but a fleshy growth of soft tissues, a web of disease and death, the cancerous, uterine tumor. Thus, in order to have living perception, the traveler must avoid the polypus which negates visionary rebirth. The significance of the polypus in Blake's works usually focuses upon its cancerous destruction. However, in the process of perception, the actions of the polypus are like the actions of the hydra or sea anemone. In fact, it is interesting to observe that if, from the chart on plate 32, the Adam sphere is removed, a claw-shaped area remains surrounding the Satan sphere. Such a space closely resembles the hydra or sea-anemone with the Satan space as the body cavity and digestive track of the polypus and the claw chamber above it as the

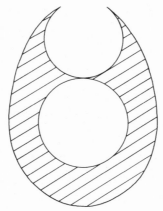

FIGURE 4. Cross-Section of the Claw Chamber as the Space
within which the Many Heads of the Polypus Revolve

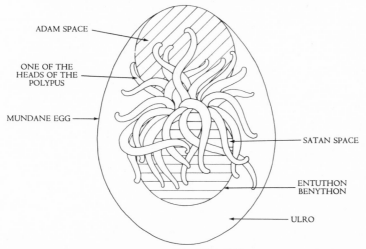

ADAM SPACE

ONE OF THE
HEADS OF THE
POLYPUS

MUNDANE EGG

SATAN SPACE

ENTUTHON
BENYTHON

ULRO

FIGURE 4a. The Vast Polypus

space within which the many heads of the polypus revolve (Figure 4). The
polypus embodies the bisexual (or asexual) vegetable world, the "Twofold
form Hermaphroditic and the Double-sexed, / The Female-male and the
Male-female, self-dividing" which stands "glorious upon the deeps of Entu-
thon." That the polypus can consume the visionary world, its physiological
analogue within the eye certainly demonstrates. In a cross-section diagram of
the eye, the cornea appears to be the body of the polypus; and the iris, which
envelops the lens with its finger-like projections, seems to be like the tentacles

of a sea-anemone closing out light (Figures 5 and 6). And Blake tells us that Golgonooza, the lens, "cannot be seen till, having pass'd the Polypus." Therefore, the polypus threatens to envelop the process of visionary perception, the transformative travel through the vortex. For this reason, images used for the vortex can also apply to the polypus. The waving flowers in the field of plate 31 can become the waving tentacles of the polypus/hydra/anemone. The dance of the flowers is the entrancing erotic dance designed to draw souls into the vegetable body, the very dance portrayed graphically on plates 15 and 16, or its visionary counterpart, the dance where the six females weave a figure eight, illustrated on plate 43. Therefore, the polypus is the emblem of all the attractions and lures which tempt Milton, the spiritual traveler, all ultimately compounded into the "vast Polypus" enclosing Milton's sixfold emanation, his three wives and three daughters and his six major works.

The third image for the journey, the Couch of Death, records a view of different densities within the vortex. These densities occur because of an increasing loss of consciousness, or loss of perception of life in eternity. That loss means leaving eternal perspectives, and paradoxically, dying into a redeemed eternal life. The Couch of Death image Blake clearly seems to have derived from his study of sepulchral monuments, a study which resulted in a series of drawings, and perhaps also engravings, made at the insistence of his master, James Basire. Particularly with the Couch of Death, Blake alludes to medieval transi tombs where an idealized effigy of a deceased man (the gisant), in all the ceremonial regalia due him, reclines upon the top of his tomb, in prayerful attitude, while beneath him lies a marble corpse (the transi), often worm and rat infested, dis-

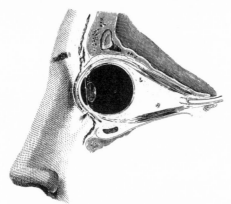

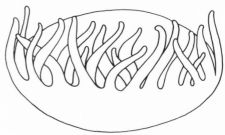

FIGURE 5. Longitudinal Cross-Section of Eye—Cornea-Iris as Polypus Embracing Lens (Golgonooza)

FIGURE 6. The Iris and Cornea of the Eye, as the Internal Polypus Enclosing the Lens as World

playing the ravages of physical corruption. Blake surely gained here the image of the Couch of Death beneath which increasingly mortal forms appear.

Milton's trip through the perceptual vortex is the active projection of a reality upon the physical world. Consequently, it follows the path of visual projection through the eye into the void. Milton steps into the vortex when he rises up "ardorous" from the eternal tables in the heavens of Albion, located upon the retina within the Adam space. (Since Albion's dead body rests on the convex surface of the lens—the Rock of Ages—everything above him might be called the heavens of Albion.) When Milton rises up, he hurls himself through the vortex of perception, through Beulah, through Albion's heart, through the polypus/iris (Entuthon Benython), down into the Ulro chaos. His path, an active projection through the eye into the void, Blake describes much as Milton described the path of Satan in *Paradise Lost*: the path is like "a trail of light as of a comet / That travels into Chaos." To leave Eden and to enter the void is to undertake a process of dying, of entering into death; it is progressive annihilation of error by entering the body of death. So Blake characterizes the process as if it were shedding life, taking off the "robe of the promise." Plates 13 and 14 record Milton's first step and the shedding process. On plate 14 Blake uses the Couch of Death to image Milton's sequential death. When Milton enters his own Shadow, he separates from his Edenic form and Blake describes it this way: "when he enter'd into his Shadow, Himself, / His real and immortal Self, was as appear'd to those / Who dwell in immortality, as One sleeping on a couch / Of gold," but Milton's Shadow "vegetated underneath the Couch." The second couch appears as the Rock of Ages where Albion lies "deadly pale." Here Milton bends down to "the bosom of death," to Albion, and Blake comments cryptically, "what was underneath soon seem'd above." The comment reminds us that death is a matter of perspective: Albion's dead body at first is below Milton, so that he is like the decayed corpse of a transi tomb; but soon Milton's dead body is below Albion, and Milton becomes the decayed corpse. A third couch is Satan's Couch in Udan-Adan with sin on the right, death on the left, and Chaos beneath. Milton's temptation, to become a "covering" for Satan, to do Satan's will, echoes the configuration of the transi tomb. The fourth couch is the Couch of Death in the physical world, where Milton's mortal portion, that "body / Which was on earth born to corruption" is the Rock Sinai, and his sixfold emanation, as the rocks of Horeb, range around him or rather above him, since the rock Sinai is in Ulro and the rocks of Horeb are in Entuthon Benython. Thus, the four couches are stages of perceptual projection of mental reality upon the world: the retina (Eden); the lens (The Rock of Ages); the focal point (Satan's Seat); and the phenomenal world of perceived objects (Ulro). These stages are the increasing intensity of error which Milton must enter, and likewise shed, to turn his vision inward, back toward Eden. But the Couch of Death image also conveys one of Blake's most essential concepts about spiritual travel, that "God himself enters Death's Door always with those that enter, / And lays down in the Grave with them in Visions of Eternity, / Till they awake & see Jesus." Therefore, when the Eternals (Ololon) in their wrath rend the heavens around Milton's couch in Eden, the "Eight Immortal Starry-Ones" "close up the Couch," flee into Ulro and guard the Couch in flaming fires. The eight watchers will protect the Couch, until Milton cleanses "the face" of his spirit to see eternity anew.

Blake's vision of the lark is his fourth major image of the spiritual journey. At the moment of redemption in *Milton* the lark mounts to the Crystal Gate, providing a beautiful image of the redemption of the perceptual process. The Crystal Gate is at the outer edge of the crystalline lens in the perceptual diagram. The lens, as we have stated, is an egg-shaped microcosm for the greater Mundane Egg that encloses the Adam and Satan spaces, which are, Blake writes, "States Created into Twenty-seven Churches." The purpose of the lark's flight is to redeem the "Twenty-seven Heavens and all their Hells," the "twenty-seven-folds of opakeness" which are "enlarg'd into dimension & deform'd" into the "indefinite space" of the Mundane Shell. Blake, in fact, tells us that the Mundane Shell "finishes where the lark mounts." The lark, as Los's messenger, rises to the Crystal Gate of the lens and arrives at "that bright Gate" where he is met by another lark. The two larks touch their wings back to back and tip to tip, and then each returns to his respective earth where each consults with Angels of Providence "all night in slumbers / Inspired." Then, in the morning, each earth or Church sends out another lark into another Heaven. The flight of the larks is very difficult to visualize unless related to the physiology of the eye (Figure 7). The lens is composed of concentric layers like an onion. Blake has visualized each layer as an earth's surface above which is a cavity or heaven. These layers are translucent; they open both within and without to other layers or earths. The flight of each pair of larks thus takes place in the spaces or heavens between the layers. Two larks rise up, from their respective layers, meet, touch their wings, and descend to their respective earths or layers. The next morning—for the lens, does the sun set and rise with each blink of the eye?—another two larks fly out from their respective earths, and so on through twenty-seven layers. The larks, in this pattern, establish a chain of communication. Touching their wings, they carry Los's news of Ololon's coming to the twenty-seven churches, and they bear the inspired truth from the respective churches back to Los. Gradually, the larks penetrate all twenty-

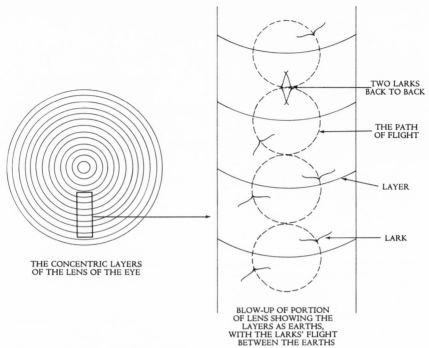

TWO LARKS
BACK TO BACK

THE PATH
OF FLIGHT

LAYER

LARK

THE CONCENTRIC LAYERS
OF THE LENS OF THE EYE

BLOW-UP OF PORTION
OF LENS SHOWING THE
LAYERS AS EARTHS,
WITH THE LARKS' FLIGHT
BETWEEN THE EARTHS

FIGURE 7. The Flight of the Larks

seven heavens—a gradual redemption of the churches and a cleansing of the lens—until their chain extends from and to their starting point, the lark's nest, where the twenty-eighth lark as Los's messenger flies to Ololon. This "Twenty-eighth bright / Lark" communicates all the news to Jesus, who is "coming in the Clouds of Ololon" to Blake's garden in Felpham. Through the flight of the larks, Blake magnificently modifies the image of St. John's Apocalypse where Jesus testifies to the churches. Blake's churches, the larks, also testify to Jesus. Not only does Blake, thereby, redeem the twenty-seven churches of Natural Religion without negating them, he announces once again that spiritual education is mutual: a church should continually renew its life in Jesus; Jesus, in turn, renews the Divine Vision within each church. Moreover, through the flight of the larks, Blake redeems John Milton's "golden chain" which connects earth to heaven in *Paradise Lost*; thus we see the fulfillment of freedom foretold in the "old Prophecy" which Los recollects: "That Milton of the Land of Albion should up ascend / Forwards from Ulro from the Vale of Felpham and set free / Orc from his Chain of Jealousy."

The fifth image of the spiritual journey is Blake's city of Golgonooza. Blake saw Golgonooza as the holy city of art through which all spiritual pilgrimages are made. When the eye is examined in cross-section, as if looking from the retina at the back of the eye toward the lens, a configuration very similar to Blake's descriptions of Golgonooza may be seen. Here, surrounded by the iris, are the domes of the lens, Golgonooza, the residence of Los and Enitharmon. The domes of the lens and the spires of the iris combine into the "mighty Spires & Domes of ivory & gold" of Golgonooza, a Gothic cathedral city of art. Thus the city of art and the medieval Christian dwelling of God are merged into one splendid image, capturing Blake's love of the Gothic interplay of worship and the use of art to decorate and celebrate the Divine indwelling. Golgonooza is, thus, the focal point of a spiritual journey, the incarnation of the word of Jesus in the prophet and his prophecy.

These remarks on the visual nature of the setting of *Milton* are presented in order to encourage the imaginative involvement of the reader's perceptual and spatial skills in understanding *Milton* and to counter the frequent allegation that Blake's spaces are so fantastic as to be incapable of visualization. We believe that Blake's concept of geography was first and foremost graphic, that each of his spaces may be seen by the visionary eye, and that such "seeing" is precisely the function of the rich detail he describes for these spaces. If the reader can overcome a tendency to see all spaces as solids and convexities, and if the reader will learn to participate imaginatively in Blake's visualization of the geography inherent in *Milton*, we believe he will enter into an exciting visionary pilgrimage which will work to cleanse his doors of perception.

THE STRUCTURE OF PROPHECY

Milton is a prophetic narrative since with it Blake exposes perceptual errors and renovates perception by teaching visionary truth. This prophetic narrative is conveyed both by words and by designs; Blake weaves together the linear orientation of words and the spatial dimensions of the graphic arts. However, in neither words nor designs does Blake adhere to orthodox sequences or patterns. That is, we can not read *Milton* "in time," from a first event to a final event. Nor can we read *Milton* "in space," from a first place to a final place. Blake structures his words and designs in intricate patterns of parallelism and inversion that lead toward the unity of all words and designs within his prophetic narration. For Blake, prophecy teaches that spiritual travel must renovate each moment of each day. The narrative in *Milton* asserts that a spiritual journey is made in time and in space, but that it simultaneously renovates our

perceptions of time and space. The journey that the character Milton under-
takes is necessarily individual, but since it shares in the archetypal pattern of
such paths, it is, as Blake confirms, mutual. Moreover, for Blake, all spiritual
journeys begin and end in the love and mercy of Jesus, the Saviour, and the
Saviour's love and mercy are present, not at one time and place or in one mirac-
ulous event, as a time-bound Natural Religion would have it, but present for
all times and in all places as the ever-present potential for regeneration.

In *Milton* Blake demonstrates the error of the purely linear, time-bound
cause-and-effect orientation of the fallen vision and its Natural Religion, a
religion of death perpetrated by the mills of Satan. The creed of such a religion
asserts that the fallen state of man's life is a punishment for sin; as a conse-
quence of this original sin man fears death, believing that at the time his first
parents fell, he, too, was condemned. Moreover, he fears that during his life
his actions will be measured and computed by Divine Justice, as Tirzah "num-
bers with her fingers every fibre ere it grow." Just as John Milton's God, in
Paradise Lost, circumscribes "the Universe, and all-created things" with his
"golden compasses"—an image Blake illustrated vividly as the Frontispiece to
Europe: A Prophecy—so man must consent to the circumscriptions of Divine
Justice, by being obedient, meek, and virtuous, fearing God and his wrath.
Knowing that Salvation will come eventually as a reward for clean living, but
that not all will be deemed worthy, man engages in religious competition for a
place in Heaven. A corporeal war is waged between the Elect and the Redeemed,
while the Reprobate are condemned to everlasting punishment, and are thereby
negated from existence. The "four iron pillars of Satan's Throne— / Tem-
perance, Prudence, Justice, Fortitude, the four pillars of tyranny" lead in-
evitably to "Religion hidden in War / Nam'd Moral Virtue." This very
religion, Blake felt, John Milton offered in *Paradise Lost* as "exemplary to a
nation."

Blake's horror at such a religion was due to its negation of love and mercy,
negation of any potential for a creative human life, for the spiritual journey.
Established upon a curse, constructed upon a system of sacrifice and offerings,
Natural Religion and the teachers of its false doctrines even made Jesus, "the
image of the Invisible God," its "prey: a curse, an offering, and an atonement /
For Death Eternal." Subsequently, this Natural Religion sought its emblems
in the miracle of virgin birth, the cruelty of the crucifixion, the life and death
of Christ in the natural body, as its doctrine "Christ took on Sin in the Virgin's
Womb, & put it off on the Cross" symbolizes. The followers of Natural Re-
ligion cry "Shew us Miracles," and through the miracle of Christ's incarnation
and atonement, they deceive themselves, hoping to rationalize their own sense

of sin. This is the major temptation of Natural Religion: the deception that we can be saved by a teacher. Blake, however, knew that salvation can only be individual: "one must die for another throughout all Eternity." To Blake, the value of Christ was not his historical appearance in time and space, but his eternal life, which continually affirms love and mercy.

Before the "dull round" of time can be annihilated, it must first be recognized. This occurs in *Milton* through the static repetition of representation after representation of "dark Satanic death," a cycle beginning with Satan, and revolving through Elynittria, Leutha, Milton's Shadow, the Sixfold Emanation, the Shadowy Female, Urizen, Rahab, Tirzah, and the virgin Ololon, returning once more to Milton's Shadow, and ending at the starting point with Satan. This cycle of error is reinforced by many graphic and verbal parallels: for example, the Druidic stone trilithon on plate 4 gives way to the stone tablets of the law Urizen holds on plate 15 (only in this design Urizen's embrace replaces the capstone of the trilithon), and the rocky coasts of England and Scotland on plate 26; the three Druidic trilithons of plate b allude to the three crosses on Calvary, illustrate the text's reference to sacrifice in London, and foreshadow the sacrifice of Abel on plate 12. In this narrative structure, Blake shows that the "dull round" has pervaded history, extending through Greece and Rome, through the Old and New Testament worlds, through ancient England and Miltonic England to Blake's England. However, *Milton's* prophetic narrative also includes four narrative structures through which the error of the "dull round" may be annihilated. These exemplify the visionary truths the prophet William Blake teaches. The first of these is the two-book structure of *Milton*; the second is a three-part thematic structure; the third is a structure of six aggregate journeys; fourth is a linear structure that underlies the poem and its events. Ultimately, it will be shown, Blake redeems a rational and mechanical sense of time and space through a narrative that is both beyond and within time and space.

The two-book structure of *Milton* represents the contrary states Blake saw as necessary for spiritual progression and energetic existence. The contraries oppose the notion of duality, an either/or relationship between opposites, which inevitably results in the tyranny of one over the other, a situation, of course, pervading Natural Religion. In dualism there is no progression; there is merely a fluctuation between opposite poles. The eternal Milton's journey in Book I and Ololon's journey in Book II parallel each other and create the union of the contraries of male and female, creator and emanation, human and divine.

Blake felt that Milton had written *Paradise Lost* in a state of selfhood, with his tyrannical, dualistic attitudes deriving from that selfhood, causing him to be separated from his emanation, with that "Sixfold Emanation scatter'd thro' the deep / In torment." To Blake, *Paradise Lost* contained the history of desire "being restrained" or, as we might interpret, the history of the emanation's torment. Milton's Messiah was the "Governor or Reason" who enforced the chain of dualistic tyranny, denying the possibility of contrariety. Blake explains:

> Those who restrain desire, do so because theirs is weak enough to be restrained; and the restrainer or reason usurps its place & governs the unwilling.
> And being restrain'd, it by degrees becomes passive, till it is only the shadow of desire. (*The Marriage of Heaven and Hell*)

In *Paradise Lost* both the desire of Satan and the desire of Adam and Eve are restrained by Milton's God and Messiah acting as patriarchal governors. Blake sees that it is Milton's patriarchy, not the serpent and not Eve, which destroys Edenic, male and female love. He sees that Milton has condemned Eve's desire and has negated the feminine virtues by exalting virginity. Thus, in Blake's poem the female becomes what she beholds. She sees a powerful male restricting her; she is jealous and envious; as a result she personifies the tyrannical female will, a matriarchy weaving the web of death, the illusion of mortality, the negation of Enitharmon's web of life. She creates and weaves Satan into a Covering Cherub, a surface of false teaching which conceals the testimony of the divine vision; this covering is the negation of Ololon's garment of mercy and compassion which contains inspired prophetic words. She appears powerful, but she is ironically only the "Shadow of desire."

With desire thereby restrained, sexual relationships become a power struggle wherein each sex loses its individual identity, resulting in the hermaphroditic forms of Natural Religion which people *Milton*. To redeem John Milton's dualism, Blake, therefore, structured *Milton* in two books, with Book I being the male journey and Book II, the female journey. Since the feminine virtues of love, desire, and mercy are "the weak," Book II is shorter, "weaker" than Book I, and Ololon's journey depends on Milton's journey. Ololon does not represent a single woman. Ololon, instead, manifests the feminine in a plural form that is both female and male. Ololon mirrors Milton's image of masculine tyranny in *Paradise Lost* when, in her wrath, she drives Milton and his guardians of mercy, the Seven Angels of the Presence, from Eden. And Ololon reflects the feminine virtues of love and mercy when she fulfills her journey so that Milton may learn to love and be merciful. Her journey "in the track of Milton's course," thus, is not presented as an annihilation of error but as a confirmation of love and mercy. For this reason Ololon's journey begins with the

Divine Vision entering Ololon, the contrary of Milton's entrance into his Shadow. And, for this reason, Ololon "enters" the Couches of Death, not actively as does Milton, but with compassionate examination. Therefore, when Ololon falls prostrate before Milton's Couch and the Starry Eight, begging forgiveness for her crime, she reflects not Milton's error but the attitude of surrender Milton must adopt. As the Divine Voice tells Ololon: "Thy love depends on him thou lovest, & on his dear loves / Depend thy pleasures . . . / Behold Milton descended to Redeem the Female Shade / From Death Eternal; such your lot, to be continually Redeem'd / By death & misery of those you love & by Annihilation." For the feminine virtues of love, desire, and mercy to exist within an individual, the individual must redeem them by the continual annihilation of his selfhood, an opening to love and a redemption of the cruel religion based on Christ's crucifixion and sacrifice. Through Ololon's surrender, Milton will embody the feminine. And his moralistic perspective, which negates desire and creates twelve-year-old virgins, will be cast off as error —just as the virgin form of Ololon is cast off into Milton's Shadow at the end of *Milton*. Just as the female depends upon the male, so the male depends upon the female. For if love and mercy and desire are not redeemed within Milton, a redemption represented by Ololon's rejection of her wrathful condemnation of Milton and her willingness to openly surrender to the journey, then Milton will have no capacity for a spiritual journey.

Blake creates Ololon, therefore, to re-vision providence. Her function in Book II, the purpose of her journey, is to redeem the erroneous providence represented by Leutha, the delusory rainbow, a covenant that gives birth to death and Natural Religion. Ololon also redeems the Shadowy Female whose garments "woven of sighs & heart broken lamentations" are garments of "Cruelty," and she redeems Rahab/Tirzah who sterilizes life as she "ties the knot of milky seed." Ololon as "a river of milky pearl" and as "clouds of blood" breaks moral, sterile codes. As the "Moony Ark," the place of feminine protection, the "Garment dipped in blood" surrounding the limbs of Jesus, the loving savior, Ololon replaces the delusory covenant of death (the Covering Cherub) with the covenant of life. The mirror language of the title-page to Book II announces "Contraries are Positives / A Negation is not a Contrary," the very message which Ololon's journey mirrors for Milton and for readers of Blake's poem. Plate 42 of *Milton* shows the eagle of prophecy calling the lovers, the contraries, to view their sexual love humanly, not moralistically, that their rock-bound position at the edge of the "sea of time and space" will not become a "Death Couch" but a foundation for regeneration of the "sexual garments" into "Human Lineaments."

Blake also stresses the contrary states in the narrative's three-part thematic pattern. The three divisions (more or less equal in length, depending upon which copy of *Milton* is read) have overlapping implications. These divisions depict the three stages of a spiritual journey, the three thematic divisions of *Paradise Lost*, and Milton's three classes of men in *Paradise Lost*. Milton called his three classes of men the Elect, the Reprobate, and the Redeemed. In these labels Blake felt Milton concealed the forms of Satan, Sin, and Death. Blake has the three divisions reflect his three classes of men which he, like Milton, calls the Elect, the Reprobate, and the Redeemed. Unlike Milton, Blake's three classes are not judgmental or dualistic; they are the two contrary states (the Redeemed and the Reprobate) and the negation (the Elect).

The first thematic division is the Bard's Song. The Bard shows Milton his error, recognition of which is the first step Milton must take on his journey. Since Milton's error is especially evident within the first division of *Paradise Lost*, where sin is created from Satan's revolt and subsequent fall from Heaven, the Bard revises Milton's narrative. He transforms sin into error. As the Bard tells it, Satan's error is a misunderstanding of his role in the divine plan. In the divine plan Satan is the agent of fragmentation and death; he is the Miller of Eternity, and his mills regulate and make distinct the duration of human life, separating birth from death, youth from age, body from soul. He is, therefore, "made subservient to the Great Harvest," which is Blake's paradoxical metaphor for the continual cultivation of living form within the duration of human life. Satan, however, thinks he can improve on the plan; he thinks he can assume Palamabron's task, the wielding of the Harrow of the Almighty. The Harrow, "a scheme of Human conduct invisible & incomprehensible" to mortals, also connotes death. This death is a death of the selfhood—part of the spiritual journey—not the death of the body—the result of vengeance as depicted in *Paradise Lost*. The Harrow represents death as mercy; death as the eternal prerequisite for spiritual growth. When Satan takes over the Harrow, he threatens to replace love and mercy with his false pity and "officious brotherhood." Satan, thereby, threatens destruction of the harvest. He disrupts the eternal labors—the planting and plowing of the fields and the milling of the crops—those labors of mental cultivation which lead to the perception of the infinite in everything, and the corresponding creation of prophecy.

Although all the eternals are partially responsible for Satan's fall, Satan, himself, is elected to embody the error because he, like Milton's Elect individual in *Paradise Lost*, is guilty of hypocrisy and moral self-righteousness. Los falsely pities Satan and permits him to drive the Harrow; Palamabron, the indecisive Redeemed, similarly yields to Satan's "mildness and self-imposition." Rintrah, the Reprobate ("of those form'd to destruction"), flames in indignation above the plowed furrow and infects Satan with the false wrath of moral self-righteousness until Satan smites Thulloh. The cycle of tyranny begins. Only Enitharmon, in true pity, protects Satan by forming a Space "for the poor infected" and closing it "with a tender Moon." "All Eden" acts as a Great Assembly to consider the situation. Palamabron requests that judgment fall on Satan, but it falls on Rintrah instead. The Assembly thus acknowledges the dissimulations of Satan—and of John Milton in *Paradise Lost*. Seeming to be one of Blake's Reprobates, the destroyers of moral codes and Natural Religion, Milton/Satan actually wears the garment of the false prophet—the false tongue of "Moral Law and cruel punishments." Milton/Satan also negates the Science of Pity, since though he pretends to care for the life of man, in fact his Natural Religion creates death. In Blake's terms, wrath divided from its contrary, pity, becomes negation. The false prophet can only wrathfully condemn error; he pities and judges others to be sinful. The true prophet points out errors in "honest indignation" (*The Marriage of Heaven and Hell*), but he also honors those who err and dedicates his life to exemplify the mercy of the spiritual journey for them. Furthermore, the Assembly does not condemn Satan or Palamabron but rather Rintrah because:

> If the Guilty should be condemn'd, he must be an Eternal Death,
> And one must die for another throughout all Eternity.
> Satan is fall'n from his station & never can be redeem'd
> But must be new Created continually, moment by moment.

Satan can not be condemned or there would be no possibility for the regeneration of individual error. Palamabron can not be condemned or there would be no state of redemption. Since Rintrah the Reprobate is the strongest—of those "who never cease to Believe"—he can be judged. He is formed for destruction because his faith, like that of Job, will survive all tests. In this way, Satan is elected to the State of error. The Bard's Satan is not an emblem of eternal condemnation; he is a figure with whom each individual should identify in order to begin a spiritual pilgrimage. In other words, each of us, like Blake's Milton, must elect Satan, thereby identifying with the Satanic selfhood.

The second thematic division of Milton, from line 10 of plate 12 through the end of Book I, details the initiation of and participation in the spiritual journey, that stage which follows the traveler's recognition of error. Having recognized his error, the traveler can embrace it and cease to condemn it. In doing so, he becomes one of the redeemed. This division thus concerns, as does its counterpart in *Paradise Lost*, the creation of the world and of man, the Adam space. However, for John Milton's Eden, a beautiful, natural, eternal paradise, Blake substitutes a paradise within. For John Milton's monarchical god who acts from vengeance and righteousness, Blake substitutes a Family Divine which loves and protects the human family. And to Milton's abstract, error-free eternity, Blake opposes an aggregate of Eternals, united in Ololon, who can err but who can also repent and redeem their error. Ultimately, in this second division Blake embodies a new creation and a new creator. His creator is a fourfold protector of the Divine, creative Vision. Through the union of the Bard, Milton, and Blake with Los, the Spirit of Prophecy, the generative vegetable world is transformed into a world continually regenerated by the prophetic spirit. Los, with eternal vigilance, directs the harvest of Allamanda and the wine-press of Bowlahoola, so that the body and blood of men may be nourished by the bread and wine of the visionary imagination. When at the Gate of Luban the sons of Los, Theotormon and Sotha, "contend with the weak Spectres" and catch them in their "Net / Of kindness & compassion," they illustrate the prophetic task. These prophetic actions redeem the actions of the vegetable polypus, where the polypus ingests and devours its victims, giving them a body of death. Theotormon and Sotha, as fishers of men, give their "victims" a body of life. Similarly, Los's printing press and, by extension, Blake's *Milton* lay their "words in order above the mortal brain," to create error in order to annihilate error "as cogs are form'd in a wheel to turn the cogs of the adverse wheel."

The third thematic division, the third stage of the journey, marks Milton's entrance into the class of the Reprobate. In the "progression" of the three narrative divisions Blake provides the stages of a pilgrimage: when the traveler has elected or recognized error (first division), he can be redeemed (second division), but he needs the strength which only the Reprobate can provide (third division). The Reprobate never ceases to believe; he questions, as does the Redeemed, but he has the strength to answer; he has the strength to remain open to the recognition of error and its redemption, but he also has the ability to remain firm in his beliefs once they have been tested by the journey. Blake thought that in an imaginative person the two contraries of Redeemed and Reprobate mutually energize each other and, thus, continually annihilate the Elect, dogmatic, righteous state of mind which always threatens to negate them. John Milton, Blake thought, had seen people as being like sheep, appointed to their respective sheepfolds by the shepherd. Blake's view, in clear contrast, is individual; judgment of an individual's merit is the individual's own responsibility.

Consequently, Blake disliked the way in which Milton conceived of the fall and judgment of man in *Paradise Lost,* and his third thematic division of *Milton* counters that conception by showing that there was no fall and that judgment is individual. In *Paradise Lost,* after Eve and Adam eat of the fruit of the tree of knowledge, God punishes Satan and his legions by changing them into hissing serpents. Then, Sin and Death spread throughout the earth, and Milton's God seems to approve of their inevitable presence. Finally, Michael gives Adam a historical panorama of evil which will result from the sin of Adam and Eve; the sleeping Eve is consoled, through a dream, by God; and Adam and Eve discover their one consolation—from Eve's seed will come revenge upon the serpent. Michael's instruction to Adam and Eve includes the requisite behavior for man if he is ever to recover paradise: absolute obedience to God; submission of Eve to Adam; virtue and restraint for both Adam and Eve.

While the third division of *Milton* also concerns a fall, it is a descent made willingly by Ololon, the Eternals, not mortals, and it is a descent of the Family Divine as One Man, united with the Eternals. Thus Blake shows, not a punishing, judgmental God managing a fall, but a God who in love and mercy always descends with those who enter "Death's Door." Ololon (a "she," but also "multitudes") decides to descend, to give themselves "to death in Ulro" when they realize their error (they have driven Milton and his Watchers into Ulro). Significantly, Ololon descends in Milton's track. Since Milton has identified himself with Satan in the Bard's Song, and since Milton represents the state of annihilation or death, Ololon's journey transforms both the condemnation of Satan and the presentation of Sin and Death in *Paradise Lost.* In *Paradise Lost* Sin and Death follow in Satan's track to earth; in *Milton* Ololon and Milton follow similar tracks in order that John Milton's sense of Sin and Death may be redeemed. Moreover, Blake's Jesus, within Ololon, participates in that redemption, because Blake thought he had to counter the religion of Sin and Death represented by Milton's Messiah in *Paradise Lost.* Like Sin and Death in *Paradise Lost,* Ololon's travel in *Milton* forms "a wide road," but unlike the road of Sin and Death, Ololon's road opens to Eternity: it is a road of love and mercy, not condemnation. Moreover, Blake, unlike John Milton, refuses to condemn woman. He does condemn the idea that male and female must be involved in sexual warfare. John Milton's notion of sexual hierarchy, as we have seen, perpetuates sexual warfare. When the woman is made to be submissive to a dominant male, the "female portion" rebels and tries to gain dominance. And, when the female seed, like that of Milton's Eve, is made the implement of revenge, then the "female portion" becomes the "Loom of Death." Blake, however, makes the feminine the agent of surrender, mercy, and love—those "weak" attributes which take great strength to maintain.

Ololon, lovingly, obeys Milton, she surrenders her virginity, and she becomes a protector. Through love Milton and Ololon, masculine and feminine, wrath and pity, unite in Jesus, the "One Man," who embodies all contraries but who asks no obedience. Jesus asks only that the pilgrim undertake a spiritual education modelled upon his own life.

Blake brings the three thematic divisions together in the closing plates of *Milton* with a confrontation between Milton, Ololon, and Satan, in order to emphasize how completely he is in disagreement with Milton's view of Divine Justice. In *Paradise Lost* Milton's three classes of men were rigidly divided: the Elect would be saved, the Redeemed might be saved, the Reprobate would be condemned. Blake sees these three classes as Satan, Sin, and Death, and he reforms them through Satan, Ololon, and Milton. Here, in *Milton*, Satan is no creeping serpent; he is both "a Twenty-seven-fold mighty Demon / Gorgeous & beautiful" and "a ruin'd Man"; Sin is not a female dragon "foul in many a scaly fold" (*Paradise Lost*), but instead "a Virgin of twelve years"; Death is not a shapeless, black shadow but a Puritan divine "clothed in black, severe & silent," of "impregnable strength." In these depictions Blake demonstrates the power of human error, not the power of a tyrannical, dehumanizing god. For, Blake believes that it is by recognizing the strong temptations within Natural Religion—Satan, Sin, and Death—that we cast off their erroneous might. Blake returns his narrative, then, to his beginning where the Bard's words offered salvation. "Three Classes are Created," and in that creation Blake transforms the "dull round" of Natural Religion that Milton so powerfully portrayed in *Paradise Lost* into the spiritual cycle of the Great Harvest.

There is a narrative structure of six parallel journeys within *Milton*, including the journeys of the Bard, Milton, Ololon, Los, Blake, and Jesus. Through these journeys Blake shows that all spiritual journeys—past, present, and future—merge within Jesus, just as the pilgrimages of *Milton* culminate within Jesus in Blake's garden at Felpham. Therefore, each of the travelers follows a path derived from the spiritual apprenticeship undertaken by Jesus. In his apprenticeship Jesus recognized and embraced his divine identity through an epiphany experience. Then, Jesus strengthened his divine identity by undergoing temptation during forty days in the wilderness. Finally, Jesus with awareness of Satan, his adversary, and in full confidence of his divinity, asserted his identity and undertook his ministry. Jesus' apprenticeship is the prototypical journey for the prophet. The prophet incarnates Jesus' spiritual path, discovers his own Human Form Divine, and is then prepared to incarnate the words of Jesus.

To use another analogue, *Milton* is Blake's vision of Pentecost, that feast of the harvest where inspired utterance takes on intelligible form. Just as Jesus descended to the disciples giving his spirit that they might continue his work, so Jesus descends to Blake's Felpham garden that his words and life might be given living form in Blake's prophecy and in all readers of Blake.

A linear structure underlies *Milton*, a kind of deep structure, which tells the autobiographical story of William Blake's reading of John Milton's works. In other words, this is the "track" of Milton to Blake, which Blake indicates graphically on plate 32. The story may be constructed in this way: Blake reads Milton in Lambeth. (Milton enters the Satan space on plate 32, Blake's world.) Blake, at first, allows Milton to impose on him, as Satan imposes on Palamabron in the Bard's Song. Then Blake becomes angry at Milton and wants to condemn him for his Natural Religion. But Blake senses that he might be judging Milton wrongfully, that in judging Milton for his sins he might be overlooking Milton's virtues. (This is the inspiration from the Bard within Blake.) Thus, Blake opens to Milton. (Milton descends as a star to Blake's foot, altering, as it has been said, "Blake's stance.") Blake, then, begins to recognize Milton's errors. (He sees the "vast breach of Milton's descent.") Consequently, Blake begins his own spiritual journey. (He binds on the pilgrim's sandal.) Blake goes to Felpham and begins to write *Milton*. (Los descends to Blake in Lambeth, immediately after Milton's descent as a star, and takes Blake to Felpham.) Blake gradually gains confidence as a poet/prophet, but his constant temptations are his own feelings of inadequacy (self-pity), a tendency to let Milton and poetic tradition dominate him (as Palamabron allows Satan to impose on him in the Bard's Song), and wrath (as Palamabron and Rintrah wish Los to destroy Milton in plate 20). However, Blake faces and overcomes these weaknesses. (Los, in joining with Blake has given him strength.) Blake is inspired; he begins to understand his own views of creation. (Los takes Blake to Golgonooza, Allamanda, and Bowlahoola.) Blake has begun to understand his role as a poet/prophet through reading John Milton's works.

Still, Blake has not finished his own poem; he has not been able to unify his ideas. He is distracted from his task by the natural beauty of Felpham, and perhaps by his wife, Catherine, and his patron, William Hayley, who urge him to turn his energies toward an occupation more profitable than visionary poetry. Suddenly, one day as he is walking in his garden at Felpham, smelling the wild Thyme, seeing a lark flying toward the clouds over his head (Ololon is descending into the garden), Blake has an epiphany. Blake understands Milton's errors and the ways in which identical errors have been restricting his own imagination. (Blake, at first, welcomes the twelve-year-old virgin, Ololon, into his garden, and sees Milton—in his second descent to Blake—as a strong and severe Puritan.) Blake refuses to condemn Milton. He will not write a poem which will negate Milton's works for his own benefit. (Milton refuses to annihilate Satan.) Rather, Blake will recognize and annihilate his own selfhood. (Blake stands in Satan's bosom.) Blake has examined his own motives. (Like Milton, he has cleansed his perception "by Self-examination.") Blake knows that he loves Milton. (Ololon descends into the garden a second time as a "Moony Ark.") Blake knows the meaning of spiritual friendship, and that with Milton he participates in a Brotherhood of Prophets. (The "Fires of Intellect" rejoice "Around the Starry Eight" in "Felpham's Vale.") Blake dedicates his poetry and his life to the Divine Vision. (The Starry Eight become "One Man, Jesus the Saviour.") Thus, Milton ends where it begins, with Blake's visionary perception of the meaning of prophecy. Only at the end of Milton does Blake realize the dimensions of the events Milton records; only at the end of Milton does Blake become the prophetic narrator of Milton; only at the end of Milton does Blake actually begin to write Milton.

Although the linear story is inadequate to Blake's vision, recognizing it does demonstrate the spirit within which Blake wrote Milton. Any understanding of John Milton enriches Milton, especially knowledge of Paradise Lost which, as Blake indicates by his epigraph, influenced the composition of Milton, although Blake's poem seems to embody Milton's Nativity Ode, his Comus, L'Allegro, Il Penseroso, Paradise Regained, and Samson Agonistes—a sixfold emanation. Blake did love John Milton, seeing in him a true poet, a prophet, a Christian artist; and, as a consequence, Blake devoted much of his life and creative effort to communication with John Milton through his many illustrations of Milton's works. John Milton was a spiritual friend with whom Blake often agreed. But in true friendship, Blake likewise opposed some of Milton's ideas, feeling that in Paradise Lost particularly, Milton had let his Satanic Selfhood dominate his imaginative spirit. Blake's task then, as a reader of John Milton's work was to recognize a potential error in his own perception. He could become angry with Milton and refuse to read him, thus negating within his own experience Milton and his ideas. But to do so would be to accuse, judge, and take revenge upon Milton, according to the limited vision of Natural Religion. Instead, Blake placed himself in his poem as an example of the loving reader who, rather than negating the great John Milton, opened himself, sacrificing his selfhood, to receive Milton's wisdom. Milton should be read, therefore, in the light of John Milton's poetry. And Paradise Lost or any of Milton's works will be enriched by Blake's Milton. Blake's goal in Milton is not to supplant or replace Milton, nor indeed to imitate or parody him. But, through the true friendship of opposition, the burning fires of thought, Blake provokes the redemption of John Milton. Blake has, therefore, revised the usual linear sense of literary history, with the earlier poet influencing and serving as master for the later poet, and the later poet surpassing or mastering his teacher. For Blake, literary influence is like a spiritual journey, a mutual conversation among prophets with "each in each & clearly seen / And seeing" (*Jerusalem*).

By the linear pattern underlying *Milton*, Blake confirms the essence of human life within time and space. Man's linear life does not have to be a "dull round of probabilities and possibilities"; the time of linear life can be filled instead with "what we should say was impossible if we did not always see it before our eyes" (*A Descriptive Catalogue*). Such is the living potential of spiritual travel and such the prophetic narrative which protects it.

William Blake, the author in whom *Milton*'s narrative originates, is one member of a Brotherhood of Prophets—the Bard, Milton, Los, Ololon and Jesus—all of whom participate in the spiritual pilgrimage into the Ulro and, subsequently, create *Milton*. Each member of the Brotherhood is at once individual and familial, which is to say that each maintains his identity, but that each by spiritual friendship unites with the Brotherhood, and with the eternal form of Brotherhood, the Starry Eight within Jesus. Brotherhood, therefore, is a mutual relationship, not a hierarchical relationship. There is no jealousy or envy among spiritual friends, no desire to surpass or eclipse the reputation of a predecessor. Rather, there is mutual communication, each to each, and a mutual support for the eternal perspectives inherent in each.

Within the Brotherhood of Prophets Blake includes both the Bard and Los, defining by these two characters, especially, his view of prophecy. The Bard in *Milton* is a singer and a storyteller. He represents the ancient Bards who inhabited a time or culture in which the divine vision was honored. The Bard sings "according to the inspiration of the Poetic Genius." His words should need no interpretation, no defense, and no justification. Those to whom he sings should recognize his songs as eternal visions of truth. Because the Eternals lack the wisdom and vision to respond to the Bard, they doubt him and cause him to take "refuge in Milton's bosom." Thus, Blake shows that the Bard's vision must be protected in times of trouble by the prophet. Los is the prophet who protects the Bard in a culture which has lost the divine vision—thus his name may be sounded "loss." The prophet, therefore, may sing songs, tell stories, and write poems. He presents the divine vision, but he must always defend it, explain it, and teach his audience how to perceive it. Los, Milton, and the Starry Eight are the teachers within the Brotherhood of Prophets. Ultimately, it is William Blake who unites both the "Divine Revelation" of the Bard and the "Litteral expression" of prophecy within his poem *Milton*, that all his readers may become prophets.

RECOMMENDED READING

Blake Studies: a semi-annual journal of scholarship and criticism. Published independently at Memphis State University, Department of English, Memphis, Tennessee 38152. [especially Volume 6, number 1, a *Milton* issue.]

Bentley, G. E., Jr. *Blake Records*. Oxford: The Clarendon Press, 1969.

———. *Blake Books*. Oxford: The Clarendon Press, 1977.

Bloom, Harold. *Blake's Apocalypse: A Study in Poetic Argument*. New York: Doubleday and Co., 1965.

Curran, Stuart and Joseph Anthony Wittreich, Jr., eds. *Blake's Sublime Allegory: Essays on The Four Zoas, Milton and Jerusalem*. Madison, Wisconsin: The University of Wisconsin Press, 1973.

Davis, Michael. *William Blake: A New Kind of Man*. Berkeley: The University of California Press, 1977.

Erdman, David V. *Blake: Prophet Against Empire*. Revised Edition. Princeton, New Jersey: Princeton University Press, 1969.

Essick, Robert N. *The Visionary Hand: Essays for the Study of William Blake's Art and Aesthetics*. Los Angeles: Hennessey and Ingalls, Inc., 1973.

Fox, Susan. *Poetic Form in Blake's Milton*. Princeton, New Jersey: Princeton University Press, 1976.

Frye, Northrop. *Fearful Symmetry: A Study of William Blake*. Princeton, New Jersey: Princeton University Press, 1947.

Grant, John E., and David V. Erdman, eds. *Blake's Visionary Forms Dramatic*. Princeton, New Jersey: Princeton University Press, 1970.

Howard, John. *Blake's Milton: A Study in the Selfhood*. Rutherford, New Jersey: Fairleigh Dickinson University Press, 1976.

Wagenknecht, David. *Blake's Night: William Blake and the Idea of Pastoral*. Cambridge, Massachusetts: The Belknap Press of Harvard University Press, 1973.

Wittreich, Joseph Anthony, Jr. *Angel of Apocalypse: Blake's Idea of Milton*. Madison, Wisconsin: The University of Wisconsin Press, 1975.

APPENDIX: Additional Plates

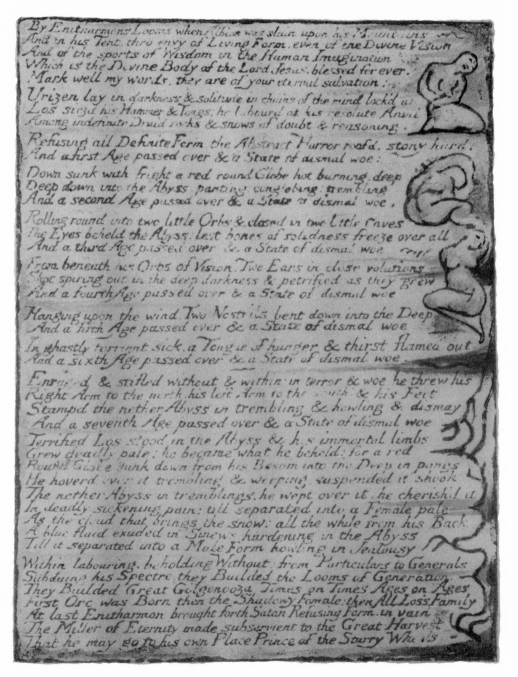

By Enitharmons Looms when Thiel was slain upon his Mountains
And in his Tent. thro envy of Living Form. even of the Divine Vision
And of the sports of Wisdom in the Human Imagination
Which is the Divine Body of the Lord Jesus. blessed for ever.
Mark well my words. they are of your eternal salvation:

Urizen lay in darkness & solitude in chains of the mind lockd up
Los siezd his Hammer & Tongs. he labourd at his resolute Anvil
Among indefinite Druid rocks & snows of doubt & reasoning.

Refusing all Definite Form the Abstract Horror roof'd. stony hard.
And a first Age passed over & a State of dismal woe:

Down sunk with fright a red round Globe hot burning. deep
Deep down into the Abyss. panting: conglobing: trembling
And a second Age passed over & a State of dismal woe.

Rolling round into two little Orbs & closed in two little caves
The Eyes beheld the Abyss. lest bones of solidness freeze over all
And a third Age passed over & a State of dismal woe.

From beneath his Orbs of Vision. Two Ears in close volutions
Shot spurting out in the deep darkness & petrified as they grew
And a fourth Age passed over & a State of dismal woe

Hanging upon the wind. Two Nostrils bent down into the Deep
And a fifth Age passed over & a State of dismal woe

In ghastly torrent sick. a Tongue of hunger & thirst flamed out
And a sixth Age passed over & a State of dismal woe.

Enraged & stifled without & within: in terror & woe he threw his
Right Arm to the north his left Arm to the south & his Feet
Stampd the nether Abyss in trembling & howling & dismay
And a seventh Age passed over & a State of dismal woe

Terrified Los stood in the Abyss & his immortal limbs
Grew deadly pale; he became what he beheld: for a red
Round Globe sunk down from his Bosom into the Deep in pangs
He hoverd over it trembling & weeping. suspended it shook
The nether Abyss in tremblings. he wept over it. he cherishd it
In deadly sickening pain: till separated into a Female pale
As the cloud that brings the snow: all the while from his Back
A blue fluid exuded in Sinews hardening in the Abyss
Till it separated into a Male Form howling in Jealousy

Within labouring. beholding Without. from Particulars to Generals
Subduing his Spectre, they Builded the Looms of Generation
They Builded Great Golgonooza Times on Times Ages on Ages
First Orc was Born then the Shadowy Female: then All Loss Family
At last Enitharmon brought forth Satan Refusing Form. in vain
The Miller of Eternity made subservient to the Great Harvest
That he may go to his own Place Prince of the Starry Wheels

PLATE a, PLATE 3 in Copy D

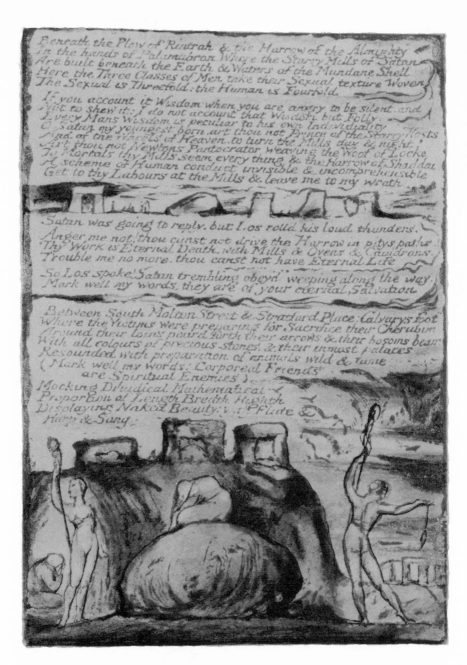

Beneath the Plow of Rintrah & the Harrow of the Almighty
In the hands of Palamabron. Where the Starry Mills of Satan
Are built beneath the Earth & Waters of the Mundane Shell
Here the Three Classes of Men take their Sexual texture Woven
The Sexual is Threefold: the Human is Fourfold.

If you account it Wisdom when you are angry to be silent, and
Not to shew it: I do not account that Wisdom but Folly,
Every Mans Wisdom is peculiar to his own Individuality
O Satan my youngest born, art thou not Prince of the Starry Hosts
And of the Wheels of Heaven, to turn the Mills day & night.
Art thou not Newtons Pantocrator weaving the Woof of Locke
To Mortals thy Mills seem every thing & the Harrow of Shaddai
A scheme of Human conduct invisible & incomprehensible
Get to thy Labours at the Mills & leave me to my wrath

Satan was going to reply, but Los rolld his loud thunders.

Anger me not, thou canst not drive the Harrow in pitys paths.
Thy Work is Eternal Death, with Mills & Ovens & Cauldrons,
Trouble me no more, thou canst not have Eternal Life

So Los spoke! Satan trembling obeyd weeping along the way.
Mark well my words, they are of your eternal Salvation

Between South Molton Street & Stratford Place: Calvarys foot
Where the Victims were preparing for Sacrifice their Cherubim
Around their Loins poured forth their arrows & their bosoms beam
With all colours of precious stones, & their inmost palaces
Resounded with preparation of animals wild & tame
(Mark well my words! Corporeal Friends
     are Spiritual Enemies)
Mocking Druidical Mathematical
Proportion of Length Bredth Highth
Displaying Naked Beauty, with Flute &
Harp & Song.

PLATE b, PLATE 4 in Copy D

174

Palamabron with the fiery Harrow in morning returning
From breathing fields, Satan fainted beneath the arrows
Christ took on Sin in the Virgins Womb, & put it off on the Cross
All pitied the piteous & was wrath with the wrathful & I Los
heard it.

And this is the manner of the Daughters of Albion in their beauty
Every one is threefold in Head & Heart & Reins & every one
Has three Gates into the three Heavens of Beulah which shine
Translucent in their Foreheads & their Bosoms & their Loins
Surrounded with fires unapproachable: but whom they please
They take up into their Heavens in intoxicating delight
For the Elect cannot be Redeemd, but Created continually
By Offering & Atonement in the cruelties of Moral Law
Hence the three Classes of Men take their fix'd destinations
They are the Two Contraries & the Reasoning Negative.

While the Females prepare the Victims. the Males at Furnaces
And Anvils dance the dance of tears & pain. loud lightnings
Lash on their limbs as they turn the whirlwinds loose upon
The Furnaces, lamenting around the Anvils & this their Song

Ah weak & wide astray! Ah shut in narrow doleful form
Creeping in reptile flesh upon the bosom of the ground
The Eye of Man a little narrow orb closd up & dark
Scarcely beholding the great light conversing with the Void
The Ear, a little shell in small volutions shutting out
All melodies & comprehending only Discord and Harmony
The Tongue a little moisture fills, a little food it cloys
A little sound it utters & its cries are faintly heard
Then brings forth Moral Virtue the cruel Virgin Babylon

Can such an Eye judge of the stars & looking thro its tubes
Measure the sunny rays that point their spears on Udanadan
Can such an Ear filled with the vapours of the yawning pit.
Judge of the pure melodious harp struck by a hand divine?
Can such closed Nostrils feel a joy? or tell of autumn fruits
When grapes & figs burst their covering to the joyful air
Can such a Tongue boast of the living waters? or take in
Ought but the Vegetable Ratio & loathe the faint delight
Can such gross Lips perceive? alas folded within themselves
They touch not ought but pallid turn & tremble at every wind

Thus they sing Creating the three Classes among Druid Rocks
Charles calls on Milton for Atonement. Cromwell is ready
James calls for fires in Golgonooza. for heaps of smoking
ruins
in the night of prosperity and
wantonness which he himself
Created
among the Daughters of Albion
among the Rocks of the Druids
When Satan fainted beneath the
arrows of Elynittria
And Mathematic Proportion was subdued
by Living Proportion

PLATE c, PLATE 5 in Copy D

Then Los & Enitharmon knew that Satan is Urizen
Drawn down by Orc & the Shadowy Female into Generation
Oft Enitharmon enterd weeping into the Space there appearing
An aged Woman raving along the Streets (the Space is named
Canaan) then she returnd to Los weary frighted as from dreams

The nature of a Female Space is this: it shrinks the Organs
Of Life till they become Finite & Itself seems Infinite

And Satan vibrated in the immensity of the Space. Limited
To those without but Infinite to those within: it fell down and
Became Canaan: closing Los from Eternity in Albions Cliffs
A mighty Fiend against the Divine Humanity mustring to War
Satan. Oh me! is gone to his own place, said Los, their God
I will not worship in their Churches, nor King in their Theatres
Elynittria! whence is this Jealousy running along the mountains
British Women were not Jealous when Greek & Roman were Jealous
Every thing in Eternity shines by its own Internal light: but thou
Darkenest every Internal light with the arrows of thy quiver
Bound up in the horns of Jealousy to a deadly fading Moon
And Oalythron binds the Sun into a Jealous Globe
That every thing is fixd Opake without Internal light
So Los lamented over Satan, who triumphant
  divided the Nations

PLATE d, PLATE 11 in Copy D

176

And Enormos Demon of the Waters: & Orc who is Luvah

The Shadowy Female seeing Milton howl in her lamentation
Over the Deeps. outstretching her Twenty-seven Heavens over Albion
And thus the Shadowy Female howls in articulate howlings

I will lament over Milton in the lamentations of the afflicted
My Garments shall be woven of sighs & heart broken lamentation
The misery of unhappy Families shall be drawn out into its border
Wrought with the needle with dire sufferings poverty pain & woe
Along the rocky Island & thence throughout the whole Earth
There shall be the Sick Father & his starving Family: there
The Prisoner in the stone Dungeon & the Slave at the Mill
I will have Writings written all over it in Human Words
That every Infant that is born upon the Earth shall read
And get by rote as a hard task of a life of sixty years
I will have Kings inwoven upon it & Councellors & Mighty Men
The Famine shall clasp it together with buckles & Clasps
And the Pestilence shall be its fringe & the War its girdle
To divide into Rahab & Tirzah that Milton may come to our tents
For I will put on the Human Form & take the Image of God
Even Pity & Humanity but my Clothing shall be Cruelty
And I will put on Holiness as a breastplate & as a helmet
And all my ornaments shall be of the gold of broken hearts
And the precious stones of anxiety & care & desperation & death
And repentance for sin & sorrow & punishment & fear
To defend me from thy terrors O Orc! my only beloved:

Orc answerd Take not the Human Form O loveliest. Take not
Terror upon thee! Behold how I am & tremble lest thou also
Consume in my Consummation; but thou maist take a Form
Female & lovely, that cannot consume in Mans consummation
Wherefore dost thou Create & Weave this Satan for a Covering
When thou attemptest to put on the Human Form, my wrath
Burns to the top of heaven against thee in Jealousy & fear.
Then I rend thee asunder, then I howl over thy clay & ashes
When wilt thou put on the Female Form as in times of old
With a Garment of Pity & Compassion like the Garment of God
His Garments are long sufferings for the Children of Men
Jerusalem is his Garment & not thy Covering Cherub O lovely
Shadow of my delight who wanderest seeking for the prey

So spoke Orc when Oothoon & Leutha hoverd over his Couch
Of fire in interchange of Beauty & Perfection in the darkness
Opening interiorly into Jerusalem & Babylon shining glorious
In the Shadowy Females bosom Jealous her darkness grew
Howlings filld all the desolate places in accusations of Sin
In Female beauty shining in the unformd void & Orc in vain
Stretchd out his hands of fire. & wooed they triumph in his pain

Thus darkend the Shadowy Female tenfold & Orc tenfold
Glowd on his rocky Couch against the darkness: loud thunders
Told of the enormous conflict. Earthquake beneath: around
Rent the Immortal Females, limb from limb & joint from joint
And moved the fast foundations of the Earth to wake the Dead
Urizen. emerged from his Rocky Form & from his Snows

PLATE e, PLATE 20 in Copy D

And Milton ris: sat up on the Couch of Death, & oft conversed
In vision & dream beatific with the Seven Angels of the Presence

I have turned my back upon these Heavens builded on cruelty
My Spectre still wandering thro' them follows my Emanation
He hunts her footsteps thro' the snow & the wintry hail & rain
The idiot Reasoner laughs at the Man of Imagination
And from laughter proceeds to murder by undervaluing calumny

Then Hillel who is Lucifer replied over the Couch of Death.
And thus the Seven Angels instructed him & thus they converse.

We are not Individuals but States: Combinations of Individuals
We were Angels of the Divine Presence: & were Druids in Annandale
Compelld to combine into Form by Satan, the Spectre of Albion.
Who made himself a God &, destroyed the Human Form Divine
But the Divine Humanity & Mercy gave us a Human Form
Because we were combind in Freedom & holy Brotherhood
While those combind by Satans Tyranny first in the blood of War
And Sacrifice & next, in Chains of imprisonment: are Shapeless Rocks
Retaining only Satans Mathematic Holiness Length: Bredth & Highth
Calling the Human Imagination: which is the Divine Vision & Fruition
In which Man liveth eternally: madness & blasphemy, against
Its own Qualities, which are Servants of Humanity, not Gods or Lords
Distinguish therefore States from Individuals in those States.
States Change: but Individual Identities never change nor cease:
You cannot go to Eternal Death in that which can never Die.
Satan & Adam are States Created into Twenty-seven Churches
And thou O Milton art a State about to be Created
Called Eternal Annihilation that none but the Living shall
Dare to enter: & they shall enter triumphant over Death
And Hell & the Grave: States that are not, but ah! Seem to be.

Judge then of thy Own Self: thy Eternal Lineaments explore
What is Eternal & what Changeable? & what Annihilable!
The Imagination is not a State: it is the Human Existence itself
Affection or Love becomes a State when divided from Imagination
The Memory is a State always, & the Reason is a State
Created to be Annihilated & a new Ratio Created
Whatever can be Created can be Annihilated Forms cannot
The Oak is cut down by the Ax, the Lamb falls by the Knife
But their Forms Eternal Exist, For-ever. Amen Hallelujah

Thus they converse with the Dead watching round the Couch of Death
For God himself enters Deaths Door always with those that enter
And lays down in the Grave with them, in Visions of Eternity
Till they awake & see Jesus & the Linen Clothes lying
That the Females had Woven for them, & the Gates of their Fathers House

PLATE f, PLATE 35 in Copy D

This book was set in Monotype Centaur,
a face originally designed by Bruce Rogers in 1914
as a titling font for the Metropolitan Museum
of New York, and modeled on Jenson's roman.
Display type was handset in Castellar.

Composed by Mackenzie-Harris Corporation, San Francisco.
Printed and bound by American Book-Stratford Press,
Saddlebrook, New Jersey.
Color plates printed by Lehigh Press, Pennsauken, New Jersey.
Production Manager Jan Tigner McLaren, Random House.

Designed by Hazel Bercholz and Julia Runk, Shambhala Publications.